STRONG IN THE LORD

52 Devotionals to Edify, Comfort & Exhort

ORLANDO HOLLINGSWORTH

Foreword by Dr. Bart Dahmer

Published by Innovo Publishing, LLC
www.innovopublishing.com
1-888-546-2111

Innovo Publishing LLC is a Christ-centered publisher located near Memphis, TN. Since 2008, Innovo has published quality books, eBooks, audiobooks, music, screenplays, and online and physical curricula that support the Great Commission, equip believers, and help create a positive Christian worldview. Innovo's capabilities and global reach provide Christian authors, artists, and ministries access to the world for Christ. To learn more about Innovo Publishing, visit our website at innovopublishing.com. To connect with other Christian creatives and to learn best practices for creating, publishing, marketing, and selling Christian titles, visit the Christian Publishing Portal at cpportal.com.

STRONG IN THE LORD
52 Short Articles to Edify, Exhort, and Comfort

All scripture was taken from the King James Version of the Bible. Public domain.

Library of Congress Control Number: 2025936298
ISBN: 979-8-88928-085-9

Cover Design & Interior Layout: Innovo Publishing, LLC

Printed in the United States of America
U.S. Printing History
First Edition: 2025

CONTENTS

PART 3 - EXHORT

FOREWORD

D ear Reader,

In Colossians 1:16–17, we're reminded of a profound truth:

"For by Him (Jesus) all things were created... all things were created through Him and for Him... and in Him all things hold together."

These words stretch far beyond our understanding. Who can fully grasp the vastness of Christ's creative and sustaining power? And yet, here you are, holding this book in your hands—a divine appointment orchestrated by the same God who holds galaxies together.

As a Christian publisher, I've had the privilege of witnessing many Spirit-led journeys in writing. But this book—*Strong in the Lord: 52 Devotionals to Edify, Comfort & Exhort* by Orlando Hollingsworth—stands apart. This author made a sacred promise to the Lord: to write what God placed on his heart, not for personal gain or acclaim but as a gift to the body of Christ. Under a pen name, he receives no royalties, seeks no spotlight, and has even released the copyright, entrusting the impact to God alone.

When the manuscript first reached my desk, I intended only to skim a few pages. But I couldn't stop reading. These devotionals stirred my spirit, moved me to praise, and reminded me of God's unwavering love. Every page is grounded in scripture and infused with wisdom that meets you right where you are. I commend it to you with joy and assurance—you will return to it often, and each time, you'll find something new.

In Christ's love,
Dr. Bart Dahmer
Founder and CEO, Innovo Publishing LLC

Part 1
EDIFY

"Therefore encourage one another and build one another up, just as you are doing."
—1 Thessalonians 5:11

"Iron sharpens iron, and one man sharpens another."
—Proverbs 27:15

1

PEACE FOR SUCH A TIME AS THIS

Let not your heart be troubled: ye believe in God, believe also in me. . . .
Peace I leave with you, my peace I give unto you: not as the world giveth, give
I unto you. Let not your heart be troubled, neither let it be afraid.
—John 14:1, 27

Amid turmoil and uncertainty, what does God expect of us? The simple answer is *trust.*

God never asked us to understand all things, to know the future, or to always have an answer. He knows our limitations and has made provision for this through His Word and Spirit, that we may be instructed in the things that we need to know and comforted regarding all else.

Will we trust our God as we hear of wars and rumors of wars? Will we maintain our absolute confidence in Him when the long-standing institutions of society begin to fall apart and life, as we have known it, seems to be in peril? Will our faith waver when God gives neither answer nor explanation for the perplexing events that we face in our own lives? Will He still be our shield, our fortress, our hiding place?

Beloved, when the waves pound against our fragile boat and the wind howls its threats, listen closely, and you will still hear Jesus say, "Be of good cheer: it is I; be not afraid."

> *Who shall separate us from the love of Christ? Shall tribulation, or distress, or persecution, or famine, or nakedness, or peril, or sword? As it is written, For thy sake we are killed all the day long; we are accounted as sheep for the slaughter. Nay, in all these things we are more than conquerors through him that loved us. For I am persuaded, that neither death, nor life, nor angels, nor principalities, nor powers, nor things present, nor things to come, nor height, nor depth, nor any other creature, shall be able to separate us from the love of God, which is in Christ Jesus our Lord. (Romans 8:35-39)*

Like David, we can say, "I have set the LORD always before me: because he is at my right hand, I shall not be moved" (Psalm 16:8).

So let us settle it in our hearts—we will keep our minds steadfastly on our God, and in turn, He has promised to give us perfect peace, He who is our everlasting Rock (Isaiah 26:3).

> *Now the Lord of peace himself give you peace always by all means. . . .*
> *(2 Thessalonians 3:16)*

2

A WORD TO THE WEARY

And Rebekah said to Isaac, I am weary of my life. . . .
—Genesis 27:46

Rebekah's admission of being tired of living is one that some believers can genuinely associate with. While it may sound both ungrateful and perhaps lacking in faith, it is nonetheless a sentiment that is sometimes very real, especially to those who endure long and painful trials.

In those times of deep, overwhelming weariness, well-meaning words of encouragement don't count for much. Yet would you please consider these if you, like Rebekah, are utterly weary of your life?

Consider that "No temptation has overtaken you except such as is common to man" (1 Corinthians 10:13)

This very moment, some of our brothers and sisters in Christ feel similarly at the end of their strength and endurance. They too are weary of it all and long for their trial to pass.

Consider that there is another reality

Whereas our instinct at this point is to panic, there is another reality that may be obscured by our pain at present. That reality is the presence and control of our Lord who not only promised never to leave nor forsake us but who also, Himself, is suffering with us through every moment of excruciating agony.

In all their affliction he was afflicted, and the angel of his presence saved them: in his love and in his pity he redeemed them; and he bare them, and carried them all the days of old. (Isaiah 63:9)

Consider the seasons

In the goodness and mercy of God the seasons of our lives are changing, almost imperceptibly, but changing nonetheless, for God is ever transforming us.

And let us not be weary in well doing: for in due season we shall reap, if we faint not. (Galatians 6:9)

Slowly but surely, we are moving toward the "due season."

Consider Jesus Himself

For consider him that endured such contradiction of sinners against himself, lest ye be wearied and faint in your minds. (Hebrews 12:3)

Consider that the One who is sustaining you knows firsthand exactly what you are facing:

For we have not an high priest which cannot be touched with the feeling of our infirmities; but was in all points tempted like as we are, yet without sin. (Hebrews 4:15)

The Lord is neither distant from our pain nor removed from our weariness. While on earth, Jesus lived with physical tiredness, perhaps even exhaustion. He lived with hostility, slander, hate, abuse, hardship, loneliness, abandonment, betrayal, rejection, and even what looked to men like failure.

He knew and felt the real pain of all the many thousands who thronged around Him, like sheep without a shepherd. Indeed, the pain of all mankind fell on Him.

Above all, He lived with the full understanding of the horror of sin and its consequences, hence He was grieved, He "groaned in the spirit, and was troubled" (John 11:33), He wept at the tomb of Lazarus and over the city of Jerusalem, and He was described as "a man of sorrows and acquainted with grief" (Isaiah 53:3).

Through all this, our Lord *endured*, setting an example for us of what we must do when we reach the point where it all becomes too much.

When our vision of the Lord and His ways is obscured by the weariness trying to drown us, we must endure "as seeing him who is invisible" (Hebrews 11:27). And if we do, our Lord promises to "satiate the weary soul, and . . . [replenish] every sorrowful soul" (Jeremiah 31:25).

Then comes the "due season" when we will reap "exceedingly abundantly above all that we ask or think"—*because we did not lose heart*—for God is "a rewarder of them that diligently seek Him."

Cast not away therefore your confidence, which hath great recompense of reward. For ye have need of patience, that, after ye have done the will of God, ye might receive the promise. (Hebrews 10:35-36)

Today your heart may be crying out,

Save me, O God; for the waters are come in unto my soul. I sink in deep mire, where there is no standing: I am come into deep waters, where the floods overflow me. I am weary of my crying: my throat is dried: mine eyes fail while I wait for my God. (Psalm 69:1-3)

If so, beloved, know that the Lord hears you, and in love He reminds you,

But they that wait upon the LORD shall renew their strength; they shall mount up with wings as eagles; they shall run, and not be weary; and they shall walk, and not faint. (Isaiah 40:31)

3

PAIN

Why is my pain perpetual and my wound incurable, which refuseth to be healed? —Jeremiah 15:18

Pain is both common to humanity and universally unwanted. No normal person desires pain, and most of us are grieved to see others suffering in its grip. Yet, for the child of God, pain has a very particular and unique function.

Now no chastening for the present seemeth to be joyous, but grievous: nevertheless afterward it yieldeth the peaceable fruit of righteousness unto them which are exercised thereby. (Hebrews 12:11)

For us who are Christ's, the purpose of pain is to enable us to bear fruit—the fruit of the Spirit, which is the very character of Christ. For us, pain is not purposeless suffering. It is not even just the common result of the sin of our race. It is the instrument of God, training us for "afterward."

Does that make it any less painful? No. But we have the peace of knowing that in it, God is at work, conforming us to the well-pleasing image of His Son, so that we may be fit to reign with Him through the millennium and for eternity.

Pain has a way of blinding us to everything other than the searing discomfort of the present. We must bring every thought into captivity to the obedience of Christ and know that there will be a glorious "afterward."

Who are kept by the power of God through faith unto salvation ready to be revealed in the last time. Wherein ye greatly rejoice, though now for a season, if need be, ye are in heaviness through manifold temptations: that the trial of your faith, being much more precious than of gold that perisheth, though it be tried with fire, might be found unto praise and honour and glory at the appearing of Jesus Christ. (1 Peter 1:5-7)

For I reckon that the sufferings of this present time are not worthy to be compared with the glory which shall be revealed in us. (Romans 8:18)

For which cause we faint not; but though our outward man perish, yet the inward man is renewed day by day. For our light affliction, which is but for a moment, worketh for us a far more exceeding and eternal weight of glory; while we look not at the things which are seen, but at the things which are not seen: for the things which are seen are temporal; but the things which are not seen are eternal. (2 Corinthians 4:16-18)

If our sanctification could be achieved without pain, God would shield us from it throughout our time here; but, as our Lord experienced, pain is an inevitable part of what it means to be living in the body of the first man, Adam.

Yet, because we are also in Christ (the last Adam), every trial, every struggle, every pain is being controlled and used to fashion us into the image of Jesus, that we might be like Him who, "Though he were a Son, yet learned he obedience by the things which he suffered" (Hebrews 5:8).

Therefore, beloved, "Let patience have her perfect work, that ye may be perfect and entire, wanting nothing" (James 1:4).

4

SPIRITUAL FAILURE

For a just man falleth seven times, and riseth up again. . . .
—Proverbs 24:16

The apostle Paul wrote, "Not as though I had already attained, either were already perfect: but I follow after. . . ." Nor have we yet attained or are already perfect. That means that there will be times when, sadly, we will fall—always a painful, discouraging experience.

A genuine believer will be profoundly saddened and ashamed about his falling and will feel a deep sense of having failed the Lord.

But there is something that impacts us even more intensely than falling, and that is *repeatedly* falling—a reality familiar to many of us. With it comes the very real possibility of becoming deeply discouraged. It is also a prime opportunity for Satan to pile condemnation upon us, to the point where we are so disheartened and disgusted with ourselves that we entertain the suggestion that we may as well stay down. After all, why get up only to fail again?

Let us, therefore, settle a few rather important matters in this regard.

First, the scriptures tell us, "There is therefore now no condemnation to them which are in Christ Jesus, who walk not after the flesh, but after the Spirit" (Romans 8:1).

If we have genuinely believed on the Lord Jesus Christ as our Savior, and are therefore *in Christ*, this scripture tells us unequivocally that *we are not condemned*. Let this great truth sink in.

Second, dear child of God, our Father is not counting the number of times we fall. What matters to Him is whether we are standing *now*. Yes, we may have fallen, but we must reject the lie that we are therefore failures in the sight of God. True spiritual failure is the refusal to keep getting up.

The instant we repent in spirit and in truth of whatever sin was involved, and we determine to walk again in obedience by faith, *that moment* we are well-pleasing to our Lord.

Remember that the natural posture of the believer is that of *standing*. Whatever happens, we must keep standing—"and having done all, to stand" (Ephesians 6:13). And as long as we refuse to stay down, determined like Paul to "follow after," we are pleasing in His sight.

Third, bear in mind that our walk with the Lord is always *now*—not yesterday or tomorrow, but this very moment. We are told that we must be both "forgetting those things which are behind" and also "take[ing] . . . no thought for the morrow" (Philippians 3:13; Matthew 6:34).

It is *in the present* that we walk with our God. Leave the past in history, and accept that the future is entirely in His control. Walk in the *now* with your Lord.

For as long as we are in this body and in this crucible of sanctification, there is the possibility of stumbling and, indeed, falling, but the word of the Lord to us is not one of condemnation. What Jesus said to His weary disciples sleeping in their weakness at Gethsemane, He says to any of His who, too, may fall: "Rise, let us be going" (Matthew 26:46).

5

ON THE POTTER'S WHEEL

Arise, and go down to the potter's house, and there I will cause thee to hear my words. —Jeremiah 18:2

We often long for the Lord to speak or intervene on our behalf. We pray and plead and go on so doing, but nothing changes. We cry out to God with ever more desperation, yet there seems to be no perceptible response. We feel sure that the Lord must understand the seriousness and urgency of our entreaty, yet time passes, and the whispers of doubt begin to grow louder until they are screams of, *Where is thy God?*

Child of God, here is an invitation to you like that "which came to Jeremiah from the Lord, saying: "Arise, and go down to the potter's house, and there I will cause thee to hear my words." The divine Potter is calling you near to witness something that few ever see and to hear words that only a handful could understand. Jeremiah records,

> *Then I went down to the potter's house, and, behold, he wrought a work on the wheels. (Jeremiah 18:3)*

That "work" is *you*—imperfect clay in the hands of the perfect Potter, who alone is able to fashion us into the image of His Son. Even when our imperfections may seem to mar the work in the Potter's hands, He can make "it again another vessel, as seemed good to the potter to make it" (v. 4). Another vessel but in the same image.

The Lord asked Israel through Jeremiah, "O house of Israel, cannot I do with you as this potter? saith the Lord. Behold, as the clay is in the potter's hand, so are ye in mine hand, O house of Israel" (v. 6). Or as Paul wrote, "Hath not the potter power over the clay . . ?" (Romans 9:21).

Why do we think that *we* should have a say in or at least an understanding of the techniques and intentions of the Potter? Who are *we* that we should question the divine "workmanship, created in Christ Jesus unto good works" (Ephesians 2:10)?

The Lord would remind us,

> *For my thoughts are not your thoughts, neither are your ways my ways, saith the Lord. For as the heavens are higher than the earth, so are my ways higher than your ways, and my thoughts than your thoughts. (Isaiah 55:8)*

We become anxious and distracted about many things and assume that they warrant a response from the Lord. But our part is to be determined to "not [be] conformed to this world: but be . . . transformed by the renewing of your mind," remembering that, "whom he did foreknow, he also did predestinate to be conformed to the image of his Son, that he might be the firstborn among many brethren" (Romans 12:2; 8:29).

We seek information; God seeks conformation. We want to understand; God wants us to overcome. We want to see; God commands us to trust. We long for a change in our circumstances; God longs to change us through our circumstances.

Are you on the Potter's wheel? Blessed are you! For the eternal God has scooped you up out of the rest of the clay and chosen to make you like His Son.

Do not resist and mar yourself in His hands. Rather, be still and know that He is God. Let His wheel of life and circumstances spin you and whirl you around as He sees fit. It matters not, for you are quite literally in the Potter's hands, and you can be "confident of this very thing, that he which hath begun a good work in you will perform it until the day of Jesus Christ" (Philippians 1:6).

> *But now, O LORD, thou art our father; we are the clay, and thou our potter; and we all are the work of thy hand. (Isaiah 64:8)*

6

HAVE YOU HEARD THE CALL?

> *My sheep hear my voice, and I know them, and they follow me.*
> —John 10:27

Child of God, has the Lord been softly speaking to you about drawing nearer to Him? Have you felt His Spirit calling to yours? Have you felt the urge to step more fully into the light of His presence?

God's dealing with us who have believed has always been one of invitation: "Come." First, He invited us to come in faith to rest in His salvation:

> *Come unto me, all ye that labour and are heavy laden, and I will give you rest. (Matthew 11:28)*

Then, like Peter, He invited us to learn that we can trust Him for the impossible:

> *And Peter answered him and said, Lord, if it be thou, bid me come unto thee on the water. And he said, Come. (Matthew 14:28-29)*

He invites us to leave everything behind (including our will and desires) and follow Him without ever looking back:

Then said Jesus unto his disciples, If any man will come after me, let him deny himself, and take up his cross, and follow me. (Matthew 16:24)

Notice that the Lord never *commands* us to come; He only ever *invites* us. He leaves the choice to us, which helps explain His statement,

Many are called, but few are chosen. (Matthew 22:14)

From the moment Paul met the Savior and heard His call to come, he made his choice:

That I may know him, and the power of his resurrection, and the fellowship of his sufferings, being made conformable unto his death. (Philippians 3:10)

Yet you would not be alone in being hesitant about responding to the call of the Spirit to come closer to Christ. The flesh will immediately start calculating the cost and rationalizing about the alternatives, and doubt ("the sin which doth so easily beset us," Hebrews 12:1), if allowed, can clamp you where you stand.

But a choice must be made.

Will you draw closer to the light of His fellowship regardless of the opposition? Do you so desire to know Him that you count the inevitable cost as "light affliction, which is but for a moment" (2 Corinthians 4:17)? Is it true for you that "to live is Christ, and to die is gain" (Philippians 1:21)?

If you are truly Christ's, the wooing of the Spirit to come closer will never cease. That is because "God is faithful, by whom ye were called unto the fellowship of his Son Jesus Christ our Lord" (1 Corinthians 1:9).

As long as you have not completely rejected the call, He will continue to issue it, for it is for this very reason that you were saved:

For whom he did foreknow, he also did predestinate to be conformed to the image of his Son, that he might be the firstborn among many brethren. (Romans 8:29)

Nothing and no one can prevent us from drawing closer to Jesus when we turn to Him in faith. God's great blessing in our mortal lives is to transform us into the image of His Son, a work that He faithfully accomplishes as we yield to His Spirit and walk in obedience.

Have you heard the call? Then it's your move.

7

CHRONIC AFFLICTION

Look upon mine affliction and my pain. —**Psalm 25:18**

There are those who seem to experience chronic afflictions—one or more long-term trials that simply will not go away. Or a seemingly never-ending series of troubles that either overlap or string together in such a way as to create a sense of perpetual distress.

Now most of us can survive a solitary trial, which may be sharp but short. Chronic affliction, though, is quite something else, where the clouds never seem to lift, and despite much prayer, it appears that it is not the Lord's will to change the situation. It is a lonely, often overwhelming place of walls closing in and air running out. It can also be a place of satanic whispers—*Yea, hath God said?* and, *Where is thy God?*

Job spent months in just such a state of agony both in body and spirit, exacerbated by four well-meaning but ignorant friends.

Paul cried out to the Lord probably for years regarding his "thorn in the flesh" (2 Corinthians 12:7). Timothy had serious stomach problems and "often infirmities" (1 Timothy 5:23). And then there was the woman in the Gospels who had suffered hemorrhaging for twelve long years.

Long-term afflictions can have the effect of wearing us down. It is not that the trial itself is necessarily any worse today than it was yesterday, but the fact that it has gone on day after day, week after week, month after month, even year after year, generates a cumulative sense of more being added on top daily, and it is this that can become overwhelming.

So how is the child of God supposed to view such intrusive, ever-present burdens, when the Lord chooses not to remove them?

To state the obvious, no one who is of sound mind enjoys afflictions. Yet we are told in the scriptures that we must "count it all joy when ye fall into divers temptations" (James 1:2). The two do not seem to make sense when placed alongside each other. How can I consider joyful that which afflicts and causes me pain? The answer is by,

> *Knowing this, that the trying of your faith worketh patience. But let patience have her perfect work, that ye may be perfect and entire, wanting nothing. (James 1:3-4)*

One thing this explains to us is that our pain is neither random nor purposeless. Rather it is a "work" that is being performed in our spirit, a work which the Lord wants to be "perfect." To what end? So "that ye may be perfect and entire, wanting nothing."

Behind these times of pain and hardship as well as through it, God "worketh for us a far more exceeding and eternal weight of glory" (2 Corinthians 4:17). This is an *immense, eternal* work of the greatest importance—a work that will determine our role in the coming millennial kingdom. This is why we can consider it *all* joy, given the wholly unmerited and disproportionate reward awaiting us, simply for trusting God in the present.

Now while we must rejoice in the glorious outcome, we are not required to enjoy the affliction itself. Indeed, nowhere in scripture does the Lord state that He expects us to enjoy trials. An affliction is, by definition, not something to be enjoyed, or else it would cease to be an affliction. The joy is in the person and plans of our loving Father and the "very present help" of our Savior (Psalm 46:1).

Never feel guilty because you are not enjoying your trials. God does not expect you to. But be careful to genuinely rejoice in that God has chosen *you* to be made "perfect and entire," gradually changed into the image of Jesus in the character of your spirit.

In addition, think on these things…

1. We need to understand that grace is *now*.

    The reality is that what we suffered yesterday is now gone, and we will never have to suffer through that day again. And what we may suffer tomorrow is not yet here, so it can't harm us today. All we must deal with is today; to be specific, all we need to concern ourselves about is *this very moment*, and it is in that moment that our God gives grace—never for yesterday or tomorrow or later.

    Does that make this moment of suffering easy? No! Not in the least! But it does make it *a moment of grace.*

    When the Lord told Paul, "My grace is sufficient for thee" (2 Corinthians 12:9), He was not referring to the day before, nor later that day, nor during the night, nor the day to come. He meant grace for the *moment*, which is how we live in reality—moment by moment—and so that is how our Lord provides the grace (the power, strength, faith, endurance) that we so desperately need . . . moment by moment.

2. You are not and never will be alone in your trial.

    If God has chosen you to endure the fire of chronic afflictions, know that, like Daniel's three companions who were cast into the furnace of blazing fire, when the moment came, the Son of God was in that furnace with them, ensuring moment-by-moment grace until the trial was over.

3. Remember, there will be an *afterwards*.

Even if it is our death that brings it to a conclusion, it will end. The trials may change from one thing to another, but they will end:

No chastening for the present seemeth to be joyous, but grievous: nevertheless afterward it yieldeth the peaceable fruit of righteousness unto them which are exercised thereby. (Hebrews 12:11)

Yes, there is an *afterwards* of the righteous fruit of the Spirit that will be produced in you, and there is also an *afterwards* to our mortal life. This is our blessed hope.

For this corruptible must put on incorruption, and this mortal must put on immortality. (1 Corinthians 15:53)

Dear suffering brother or sister, the hand of God is upon you! In this moment, begin "looking unto Jesus the author and finisher of our faith" (Hebrews 12:2). If you can look to the joy set before you and endure by the Lord's moment-by-moment grace, before long, on that great Resurrection Day, you will be exalted to your glorious place of rulership and honor with your beloved Savior.

Chronic affliction is often the finishing school of the saints—a place of refining and preparation. Don't lose heart now. Live in your moment of grace, moment by moment in the loving presence of He who loves you and gave Himself for you.

8

FAITH FROM FIRST TO LAST

Looking unto Jesus the author and finisher of our faith. . . .
—Hebrews 12:2

It ought to be a tremendously encouraging thought that Jesus is both the author *and* the finisher of faith. That is to say, He initiates it, and He will complete it as well. All we have to do is fix our eyes on Him and follow His example and Spirit.

The Lord has not left it up to us to somehow manufacture our own faith. No, rather He gives it to us as a gift:

For by grace are ye saved through faith; and that not of yourselves: it is the gift of God: Not of works, lest any man should boast. (Ephesians 2:8-9)

This gift of salvation through faith needs first to be received and then lived in, but it is all a work of God.

Faith is the first thing. It is the fundamental thing—the foundational thing—for "without faith it is impossible to please him" (Hebrews 11:6).

We cannot come to God without faith, and we cannot walk with God and please Him without faith. But it is *He* who gives it and who perfects it, through many trials and struggles, as we take one small step after the other in following Him.

It is natural (but altogether wrong) to think that we somehow chose to trust God to start with and that by our effort we continue to do so. The truth is that *Jesus* is the author and the perfecter of faith, hence why He said,

I am the vine, ye are the branches: He that abideth in me, and I in him, the same bringeth forth much fruit: for without me ye can do nothing. (John 15:5)

Nothing!

Satan is also aware of this fact, and his one simple strategy from the Garden of Eden until this day has been to try to separate us from the Author and Perfecter by providing alternatives to absolute faith in God. He knows that it is *the shield of faith* that protects us from his attacks, so he seeks to find ways to get us to lay it down.

Never underestimate the enemy's determination to destroy or damage our faith. His assaults can be ferocious and are persistent, but so long as we maintain trust in our God, they will fail.

We, however, can grow weary and/or distracted and, like Peter walking on the water, begin to sink. Yet even then one cry for help and the Master is there to lift us up and remind us that there is never a need to doubt.

At times, in our weakness, we wonder whether we are going to make it to the end, whether we can finish this race. At such times we must recall the fact that the Author is also the Perfecter and Finisher of faith and that "he which hath begun a good work in you will perform it until the day of Jesus Christ," for "Faithful is he that calleth you, who also will do it" (Philippians 1:6; 1 Thessalonians 5:24).

For it is God which worketh in you both to will and to do of his good pleasure. (Philippians 2:13)

9

SANCTIFICATION

And be not conformed to this world: but be ye transformed by the renewing of your mind, that ye may prove what is that good, and acceptable, and perfect, will of God. —Romans 12:2

What is *sanctification?*
It is a change from the carnal to the Christ-like, a dying to self and sin and living in Christ, learning how to think like the new man and not like the old, and is entirely a work of the Spirit.

This process is of necessity a painful one because "the law of sin and death" is that which our minds have been accustomed to, whereas the Lord would have us submit to a new law: "the law of the Spirit of life in Christ Jesus" (Romans 8:2). The extent to which we are willing to pay the price to be transformed from one to the other will determine the degree to which we become like our Lord.

Sanctification is a very personal exercise, which is why the Lord allows us to have such differing experiences and levels of intensity in the trials that we face. The Potter knows His clay and the Refiner His gold. It is therefore not only wrong but dangerous to compare one believer's experiences with another's as though we were in a competition or beauty contest.

Instead, we must encourage and support one another in sanctification, knowing the struggle involved. And we can be confident both for ourselves and for them that so long as we endure to the end,

He which hath begun a good work in you will perform it until the day of Jesus Christ. (Philippians 1:6)

Sanctification includes separation from the world, its systems, its norms, and its influences, as well as disengagement from anything that does not aid the process of becoming like Jesus in our character.

Wherefore seeing we also are compassed about with so great a cloud of witnesses, let us lay aside every weight, and the sin which doth so easily beset us, and let us run with patience the race that is set before us. (Hebrews 12:1)

Indeed, there are things we have to separate ourselves from and, conversely, things we must immerse ourselves in.

The more we read and think upon the Word of God the more exposed we are to the mind and character of Jesus. In addition, when we pray in spirit and in truth, it brings us into a oneness with the Lord, otherwise inaccessible, and makes us able to see and understand things in our lives that are not like Him.

Sanctification is a quiet, almost imperceptible work of the Spirit but one that is unmistakable. There is something immensely heartwarming and thrilling about meeting another believer for the first time, yet they remind you so much of Jesus.

One day soon, when we finally meet Him face to face, I believe that for the sanctified believer, there will be the most profound and deeply humbling sense of already knowing Him—except that then, the veil will have finally been removed, and we shall see Him as He is. Hallelujah!

Perseverance through faith—that is all the Lord requires of us during this process of sanctification. He does everything else.

The question is, how badly do we want to be sanctified? What are we willing to suffer so that we might be changed into the image of Christ? Are we ready to take up our cross and follow Him into the "fellowship of his sufferings, being made conformable unto his death" (Philippians 3:10)? Each one of us must answer for ourselves.

For which cause we faint not; but though our outward man perish, yet the inward man is renewed day by day. For our light affliction, which is but for a moment, worketh for us a far more exceeding and eternal weight of glory. (2 Corinthians 4:16-17)

10

ON DISPLAY

Jesus answered, Neither hath this man sinned, nor his parents: but that the works of God should be made manifest in him. —John 9:3

When we suffer, particularly severely or in a prolonged manner, and especially when that suffering is public and cannot be hidden, we are apt to feel put upon and singled out and are tempted to think that the Lord seems uncharacteristically unfair and uncaring.

Public afflictions have the added dimension of the eyes and therefore opinions of others being focused on us at that painful and vulnerable time. And we may wonder why it had to happen like this. Why did the Lord arrange for us to be the subject of gossip, speculation, and false pity? It feels humiliating, unnecessarily so, and it does not take long for "Job's friends" to show up and "set us right," an experience that exacerbates the trial and hurts more than the affliction itself.

So why? Why would our loving Lord permit such a thing to occur in the life of one of His own? Perhaps part of the answer lies in the scripture text above.

When we suffer publicly, it is not necessarily that we have sinned and are being exposed but rather that the Lord in His sovereign wisdom has chosen us to be put on display so that, as we persevere in trusting Him despite the carnage of our experience, others may see our faith and the faithfulness of God and glorify Him to whom belongs the glory indeed.

As to why the Lord has chosen you or me and not others, this author cannot say. But this one thing is sure:

His work is perfect: for all his ways are [just]: a God of truth and without iniquity, just and right is he. (Deuteronomy 32:4)

The LORD is righteous in all his ways, and holy in all his works. (Psalm 145:17)

Paul told the self-focused Corinthians,

For I think that God hath set forth us the apostles last, as it were appointed to death: for we are made a spectacle unto the world, and to angels, and to men. (1 Corinthians 4:9)

Has God "set you forth"? Has He put you on display, on view for all to see? Then let them see that God is faithful and true and can be glorified in us under any circumstances. Even as you endure the searing pain or gnawing disappointment, or the vacuum of uncertainty, let them see Christ in you, the hope of glory.

Paul said,

For the which cause I also suffer these things: nevertheless I am not ashamed: for I know whom I have believed, and am persuaded that he is able to keep that which I have committed unto him against that day. (2 Timothy 1:12)

There was no hiding the suffering of the Son of God when the time came for Him to be offered up. As He hung there for hours, completely naked, gasping for breath, writhing in pain, taunted and abused by the Jewish religious elite, Roman soldiers, and even those who were also being crucified, His face so mangled, His body in shock due to blood loss from the horrific scouring He had endured earlier, and infinitely above all else, bearing the sin of all mankind in Himself.

Totally alone, there He hung on full display, to the glory of His Father.

If you have been chosen to be on display, let this be your "earnest expectation and my hope, that in nothing I shall be ashamed, but that with all boldness, as always, so now also Christ shall be magnified in my body, whether it be by life, or by death" (Philippians 1:20).

It is an indescribably precious privilege to be made an exhibition of God's faithfulness and grace,

> *For unto you it is given in the behalf of Christ, not only to believe on him, but also to suffer for his sake. (Philippians 1:29)*

Rejoice in this privilege, dear child of God, so that "the name of our Lord Jesus Christ may be glorified in you, and ye in him, according to the grace of our God and the Lord Jesus Christ" (2 Thessalonians 1:12).

11

BEHIND THE SCENES

And the LORD said unto Satan, Whence comest thou? Then Satan answered the LORD, and said, From going to and fro in the earth, and from walking up and down in it. —Job 1:7

Context is so important. Most words, actions, and events are meaningless at best and are prone to total misunderstanding at worst without the context that shaped them.

The context of Job's astounding afflictions was entirely spiritual, but he was not aware of that. He knew nothing of the momentous event that had occurred in "heavenly places" in the dialogue between God and Satan and that Job had been singled out as one whom Satan had set his heart upon because he "was perfect and upright, and one that feared God, and eschewed evil" (Job 1:1).

Satan, for his part, was convinced that even the best man on earth had only a transactional relationship with God and that if his blessings were removed and replaced with pain, he would turn on God in unbelief and demonstrate behavior akin to his rebellious character.

This roaming spiritual predator felt sure that God had erred in giving him access to Job and that he could deal a crippling blow to God's loving investment in mankind and prove man to be as irretrievably self-centered as he was.

And so the scene was set—a theater invisible to Job's eyes and entirely beyond his comprehension.

Remember that what was happening behind the scenes was the spiritual and unseen impacting the physical and natural. A powerful, vicious, merciless spirit being had focused all his hate on a man who had no idea that he was the subject of a spiritual test and whose only "fault" was wanting to please God.

Remember, too, that Satan challenged God about Job not once but twice (Job 1:6; 2:1), after both of which Satan attempted to implicate God as the author of Job's misery:

- The sudden and unexpected Sabean theft of Job's oxen and donkeys and the murder of his servants
- The "fire of God [falling] from heaven" and burning alive the sheep and the servants tending them (Job 1:16)
- The Chaldean theft of the camels and slaughter of the servants there
- A "great wind from the wilderness," targeting the house where all his children were meeting together, and killing them all (Job 1:19)
- Terrible "boils from the sole of his foot unto his crown" suddenly appearing on Job's body (Job 2:7)
- His wife pleading with him in despair to "curse God, and die" and friends whose ignorant words were the crowning torment (Job 2:9)

In all of this, Satan camouflaged himself well and ensured the finger of blame pointed directly at God, as demonstrated by the words of Job's wife.

Confronted by such catastrophic events, the natural mind says that even if God did not directly cause this, He most certainly could have prevented it.

In this maelstrom of unparalleled affliction, how could Job possibly have known that the eyes of heaven, as well as those of the spiritual forces of wickedness, were all focused on him? How could he have understood the epic spiritual battle involved in the circumstances he was facing?

Context. When we face deep and severe trials, we *must* remember that the spiritual mechanics of our suffering are happening behind the scenes and beyond our view. God is at work with a great and glorious purpose. The thief is also at work, having come "to steal, and to kill, and to destroy" (John 10:10).

All *we* see is the tribulation. All *we* feel is the pain. All *we* know is the loneliness of having to face something that no other human being can deliver us from. Yet from the book of Job, we learn the following:

1. God was with Job throughout all of his sufferings. God is with you, here and now, in the fire of *your* trial:

   For he hath said, I will never leave thee, nor forsake thee. (Hebrews 13:5)

2. At the appointed time, God brought Job's horrible trials to an end. Hard as it is to even begin to contemplate amid the searing pain, God has set a limit to the extent and duration of your trial:

   There hath no temptation taken you but such as is common to man: but God is faithful, who will not suffer you to be tempted above that ye are able; but will with the temptation also make a way to escape, that ye may be able to bear it. (1 Corinthians 10:13)

3. As a result of these trials, Job "saw" God as he never had before and was transformed. The pain of suffering can blind us to the magnificence of the Savior who stands with us in the fire, but once we truly *see* Him, we are never the same again.

4. In Job's case, God reversed the physical and material harm caused by Satan. Why? Perhaps because He knew that these blessings would not distract him from total attention to God, and perhaps to ensure that Satan's unjust assault upon His servant was seen by all to have been utterly futile.

In the age in which Job lived, this was the greatest reward he could have received. As a child of God and one "called according to His purpose," your reward will be infinitely greater, even if we have to wait a little longer than Job did to fully receive it (Romans 8:28).

Through this record of Job's experiences and through other scriptures, our gracious God has given us a glimpse into the spiritual world and an understanding of His sovereign majesty and eternal purposes. We see that the events of our lives are neither random nor coincidental but behind the scenes have been ordered by the Lord as specifically and perfectly as He ordered the universe, for He is working in us to perfect that "good work," which he began in you (Philippians 1:6).

For which cause we faint not; but though our outward man perish, yet the inward man is renewed day by day. For our light affliction, which is but for a moment, worketh for us a far more exceeding and eternal weight of glory; while we look not at the things which are seen, but at the things which are not seen: for the things which are seen are temporal; but the things which are not seen are eternal. (2 Corinthians 4:16-18)

12
STAND!

Wherefore take unto you the whole armour of God, that ye may be able to withstand in the evil day, and having done all, to stand.
—Ephesians 6:13

Stand.

It is the command that has been given to armies down through the centuries, and it means to hold fast and not give an inch as the enemy advances. It means do not back away, and do not give way. Absorb the enemy's onslaught, but do not buckle. Do not let him through!

For us in this long and intense spiritual battle, the Lord's unequivocal command to us is, having done everything necessary, we must *stand!*

Regardless of how often or how badly we fail, we must never give in or give up. No! Instead, we must *stand.*

Regardless of how weak we feel, how far away God seems, or how hopeless things appear, there must be no surrender. Yes, regardless of how lonely we are, or how isolated or ostracized, we must not collapse. We must *stand.*

Whatever physical, mental, or spiritual condition we may be in at this moment, we must never turn and run. We must *stand.*

What does scripture say? It speaks of "this grace wherein we *stand*" (Romans 5:2). It states that you "*standest* by faith" (Romans 11:20). It says that "God is able to make him stand" (Romans 14:4). It admonishes us to "*stand* fast therefore in the liberty wherewith Christ hath made us free, and be not entangled again with the yoke of bondage" (Galatians 5:1). It instructs us to "*stand* against the wiles of the devil" (Ephesians 6:11). It reminds us to "*stand* perfect and complete in all the will of God" (Colossians 4:12).

We must not fall away:

Now the Spirit speaketh expressly, that in the latter times some shall depart from the faith, giving heed to seducing spirits, and doctrines of devils. (1 Timothy 4:1)

We must not even look back:

And Jesus said unto him, No man, having put his hand to the plough, and looking back, is fit for the kingdom of God. (Luke 9:62)

We must *stand.*

Child of God, you may feel too beaten to fight on, but take heed to what the Lord said to the assembly at Smyrna:

I know thy works, and tribulation, and poverty, (but thou art rich) and I know the blasphemy of them which say they are Jews, and are not, but are the synagogue of Satan. Fear none of those things which thou shalt suffer: behold, the devil shall cast some of you into prison, that ye may be tried; and ye shall have tribulation ten days: be thou faithful unto death, and I will give thee a crown of life. (Revelation 2:9-10)

Stand, beloved. *Stand firm!*

13

THE NEED FOR COMFORT

Blessed be the God and Father of our Lord Jesus Christ, the Father of mercies and God of all comfort. —2 Corinthians 1:3

How we need God's comfort in this day in which we live!

These are extraordinary times of turmoil, upheaval, and uncertainty, as we witness the collapse of the foundations that supported society for so many years. We watch as the unthinkable becomes commonplace and the inconceivable becomes the norm, and increasingly we know that we are strangers and pilgrims here.

Furthermore, believers continually face Satan's increasingly subtle but vicious onslaught, as wave after wave of discouragement, deception, and distraction assail us, and at times the unrelenting struggle can seem overwhelming. Yet Christ's "little flock" remains, albeit battle-worn, beset, and often bewildered (Luke 12:32).

Thus we have this word of admonition:

Beloved, think it not strange concerning the fiery trial which is to try you, as though some strange thing happened unto you: but rejoice, inasmuch as ye are partakers of Christ's sufferings: that, when his glory shall be revealed, ye may be glad also with exceeding joy. (1 Peter 4:12-13)

Do not think it a strange thing but rather rejoice that we can partake of Christ's sufferings. Rejoice, not in the suffering but rather in "the grace that is to be brought unto you at the revelation of Jesus Christ"—

that is, the "far more exceeding and eternal weight of glory" (1 Peter 1:13; 2 Corinthians 4:17).

The Lord knows every detail of that with which we struggle, and He desires greatly to comfort us if we will permit Him.

> *For as the sufferings of Christ abound in us, so our consolation also aboundeth by Christ. (2 Corinthians 1:5)*

As we are comforted, we are also reminded of the great work of transformation that is taking place in us, and of the crown to come.

Our Lord forewarned us that, "In the world, ye shall have tribulation," and Paul reminded us that "all that will live godly in Christ Jesus shall suffer persecution." So let us indeed not think it strange.

We need the comfort of the scriptures and of the Spirit, and that which comes through the love of the saints (Romans 15:4; John 14:16; Romans 1:12).

May we allow ourselves to be comforted by God so that we may be refreshed, revived, and able to comfort others also, as we press toward the mark to finish our course with joy.

> *Now our Lord Jesus Christ himself, and God, even our Father, which hath loved us, and hath given us everlasting consolation and good hope through grace, comfort your hearts, and stablish you in every good word and work. (2 Thessalonians 2:16)*

> *Wherefore comfort one another with these words. (1 Thessalonians 4:18)*

14

A WORD OF COMFORT

In the ever-changing and unpredictable events of life, we are sometimes confronted with circumstances which, in their magnitude and/or suddenness, cause us to feel completely overwhelmed, as though suddenly thrust into a dark tunnel.

At such times we need a word of comfort from the Lord—a reminder of what is real and what is not; what is true and what is false. And a reminder of who He is.

In the Valley

Yea, though I walk through the valley of the shadow of death, I will fear no evil: for thou art with me; thy rod and thy staff they comfort me. (Psalm 23:4)

Through the seemingly endless, lonely, dark, and claustrophobic valley where faith is stretched virtually to collapse, what matters is that God is with us and will comfort us by the rod and staff of His Word and Spirit. Therefore, "I will fear no evil."

When Anxiety Threatens to Overwhelm

In the multitude of my [anxious] thoughts within me thy comforts delight my soul. (Psalm 94:19)

When no one and nothing else can help us, "Thy comforts delight my soul" (Psalm 94:19).

The Spirit of God need never be summoned or pleaded with to come to our assistance, for He is ever with us; indeed, He indwells us, being one with our spirit (1 Corinthians 6:17). And the Word of God that we have hidden in our hearts cannot be removed nor nullified by tribulation of any sort.

When Fear Stalks

I, even I, am he that comforteth you: who art thou, that thou shouldest be afraid of a man that shall die, and of the son of man which shall be made as grass; and forgettest the Lord thy maker, that hath stretched forth the heavens, and laid the foundations of the earth; and hast feared continually every day because of the fury of the oppressor, as if he were ready to destroy? and where is the fury of the oppressor? (Isaiah 51:12-13)

Indeed, who are we to hold the fear of man or anything else above Almighty God? Why should we fear man, devil, or circumstance when our Lord has said, "I, even I, am he that comforteth you"?

So, "What shall we then say to these things? If God be for us, who can be against us?" (Romans 8:31).

In Mourning

Blessed are they that mourn: for they shall be comforted. (Matthew 5:4)

Is this a promise only for the future? No! God's comfort for us who mourn is also in the here and now, for "God is our refuge and strength, a very present help in trouble" (Psalm 46:1). He desires to comfort us, never leaving nor forsaking us.

Our Lord Jesus knows the anguish of deep sadness, having been "a man of sorrows, and acquainted with grief" (Isaiah 53:3). He knows the pain of those who mourn and is Himself the comfort.

In Tribulation

Blessed be God, even the Father of our Lord Jesus Christ, the Father of mercies, and the God of all comfort; who comforteth us in all our tribulation. (2 Corinthians 1:3-4)

Ours is a merciful Father, able to comfort us in every circumstance and in all our affliction. There has never been and will never be a situation in which our Father will not be able to comfort us, assuring us of His love and anointing us with His peace.

We may not know what is before us, but we can be certain that our Lord is already there to comfort us when the time comes.

Remember . . .

The Lord desires to encourage us and teach us how to persevere in faith.

For whatsoever things were written aforetime were written for our learning, that we through patience and comfort of the scriptures might have hope. (Romans 15:4)

Unwavering trust in the Word of God produces comfort and encouragement now and perseverance over time. These cannot be acquired by any other means, and the Lord longs for us to learn this, so that we may be encouraged now and eventually grow into the image of Christ, who, "Though he were a Son, yet learned he obedience by the things which he suffered" (Hebrews 5:8).

Be encouraged as you learn obedience through perseverance.

Remember the word unto thy servant, upon which thou hast caused me to hope. This is my comfort in my affliction: for thy word hath quickened me. (Psalm 119:49-50)

God will always honor His Word, for He is "God, that cannot lie" (Titus 1:2). We therefore can have complete faith in all that He promises, even amid our worst, most crushing afflictions.

It is for this reason that there "are given unto us exceeding great and precious promises: that by these ye might be partakers of the divine nature, having escaped the corruption that is in the world through lust" (2 Peter 1:4).

I remembered thy judgments of old, O LORD; and have comforted myself. (Psalm 119:52)

15

AN ABSENT GOD?

My tears have been my meat day and night, while they continually say unto me, Where is thy God? —Psalm 42:3

There are moments when it feels as though God is distant or absent. Such experiences can be deeply confusing and profoundly discouraging, especially when our circumstances appear to contradict the promises of God.

How Can This Be Happening?

How can God say that He is our *provider*, but then we find ourselves unemployed or unable to pay our bills, despite being faithful to Him and prudent in our financial affairs?

How can God say that He is our *protector*, but then we or some loved one has a serious car accident or is the victim of some crime or act of injustice?

How can He say that He *cares* for us, but then we lose our physical or mental health, to the point where we live in constant pain or discomfort and are dependent on medication or others to survive?

How can He say that He is our *guide*, when we plead with Him for direction and seem to get none, or we follow His direction and it leads us into deep and complex trouble?

How can He say that He loves us, and yet He watches us struggle day after day with some weakness, falling into sin again and again, and never seems to intervene to give us the much-longed-for victory?

How can He be the *author* of marriage and yet allow His own to experience heartbreaking divorce?

The questions could go on and on and on.

When we think upon these things, the mind boggles, fear enfolds us like a cold shadow, the earth beneath our feet seems to give way, and our hearts cry out, *How can this be happening?!*

Lord, Are You There?

In Genesis 16 we read of Hagar who was an Egyptian maid to Sarai (Abram's wife). Assuming that she could not bear any children, Sarai gave Hagar to her husband to be his second wife with the understanding that when Hagar conceived, Sarai would take the child as her own. Under the double pressure of wanting an heir and wanting to please his wife, Abram agreed.

When Hagar conceived, her attitude to her mistress changed, and she began to despise Sarai. Consequences soon followed as Sarai badly mistreated her to exact revenge. It became so unbearable that Hagar ran away, not knowing where she was going but wanting to escape from the indignity and torment of being under Sarai's vengeful reign of terror.

It would not be unreasonable to ask where God was during all of this. Could He not have stopped Abram or Sarai from following through on the very bad idea of a second wife, or have prevented Hagar from conceiving, or at least somehow have shown her that she should not despise her mistress? Was He blind to the subsequent affliction that was meted out by Sarai on her defenseless handmaid? Was He in any way interested in this unfolding disaster?

As Hagar fled, she came to a fountain of water. Exhausted physically and emotionally, she had reached the end of the line—the limit of her strength and endurance. Now there was nowhere to go, no one to turn to, and no means to survive.

Seeing the God Who Sees You

Hagar had fled hopelessness and torment only to meet certain death with none but herself to witness her end. But she was about to discover that she was not alone. The messenger of Yahweh appeared to her at that fountain, bringing gentle comfort, instruction, and even a prophecy about her yet unborn child and his descendants. He told her to name the child Ishmael (meaning "God that hears") "because the LORD hath heard thy affliction" (Genesis 16:11).

What a revelation to Hagar!

God had heard her affliction—all of it. He had been there all along and had heard it all. Just moments before, she thought she was totally isolated, forgotten, and unseen. Now "she called the name of the LORD that spake unto her, 'Thou God seest me'" (*El Roi*, Genesis 16:13). She realized that not only was He the God who hears but also the God who sees. Indeed, the well itself where this meeting took place became known as *Beer-lahai-roi*, which means, "well of the One who lives and sees me."

Hagar was never the same again; she was a transformed woman. She went back to her mistress and submitted herself to her, bore Ishmael, and weaned him.

God Is There

Years later Hagar again had to leave that household—forced out this time—and again (now with her son) she wandered in the wilderness, came to the end of all that she had and all that she could do, and simply sat down, waiting for the death of them both. Yet once again the God who hears and sees made her know that He was present, that He had heard and seen everything, and He was able to keep His word concerning her son.

Dear reader, has God seemed absent from much of what transpires in your life? Does it appear that He has removed Himself or closed His ears or turned away His eyes? Do you feel deserted, forgotten, and unseen? Have you come to the end of your courageous battle to hang on—resources depleted, wandering in the wilderness, perhaps waiting only for death as a way out?

Then know this: *El Roi is there.*

God has heard your prayers and has seen your tears. He has seen your affliction and the unrelenting pressure. He sees your exhaustion and weakness and your efforts to try to keep trusting Him even when everything in you and outside screams, *You're on your own!*

The Lord saw everything and heard everything, and He has come to meet with you here at this well—the "well of the One who lives and sees me." It is no coincidence that you are now reading this.

When He said, "I will never leave thee, nor forsake thee" he meant it, for "God, that cannot lie, promised" (Hebrews 13:5; Titus 1:2).

He Is Not Absent

He is not even distant. God is *for* you (Psalm 56:9), *within* you (1 Corinthians 3:16), *around* you (Psalm 125:2), *beneath* you (Deuteronomy 33:27), *behind* you (Isaiah 30:21), and *ahead* of you (John 10:4).

Reject the lie of the absent God.

Even if, like Hagar, you are partly responsible for some of the trouble you are facing, remember that when the Lord met Hagar,

- there was not one word of condemnation,
- He gently and lovingly dealt with her,
- He revealed Himself as the God who heard and saw all that had taken place in her life,
- He directed her and transformed her through that encounter, and
- thousands of years later we are still talking about her today.

Only God could take a low-born Egyptian servant who had nothing left and make her a righteous example of His grace. Let Him do the same for you.

An absent God? *Nothing* could be further from the truth.

16

OFFENDED AT JESUS

And blessed is he who is not offended because of Me. —Matthew 11:6

When circumstances turn against us, it is incredibly easy to pity ourselves.

At the very least, we long for someone (anyone, really) to pity us and to acknowledge the depth and extent of what we are going through. It seems unjust that we should have to suffer so much in silence with only the Lord as a witness.

If we can't have deliverance, then we desire sympathy, not out of a deliberate desire to be seen as a martyr but rather because the pain seems too much for one person to bear in solitude, especially when there is no visible end in sight.

Have you ever been in that lonely place? Then you know the sensation of the walls closing in and that sickening, sinking feeling of hanging on in apparent hopelessness. You can almost feel the shield of faith slipping from your grasp as the cold presence of unbelief envelopes you, evidenced by fear, perhaps even blind panic, as you start seeking somewhere to run to . . . a place to hide.

Are we here describing the thoughts and actions of a spiritual coward? Not necessarily, for any of us can reach that point. Indeed, even the best of us, for how many of us would judge ourselves godlier than John the Baptist?

After all that he had suffered in preparation for the Messiah's arrival, and despite the undoubted success of his mission as His forerunner, we are presented with a sobering scene in Matthew 11 (further explained in chapter 14).

In brief, John had been unexpectedly and unjustly arrested and imprisoned, and he would later be executed there. While in prison he sends a message to Jesus in the form of a question, as devastating as it was brief:

Art thou he that should come, or do we look for another? (Matthew 11:3)

Pause and allow that to sink in for a moment. The forerunner of the Messiah sends Him a message from prison, asking, in effect, whether He is who He says He is—or is a fake.

Whether John's doubt was born of shock and disappointment at his own circumstances or (more likely) because he felt that Jesus was not doing what he expected Him to do, or not how he expected it done, or perhaps not at the speed he had hoped for, we cannot say with certainty. But what we do know is that the man who sacrificed all for Christ now seems totally disillusioned.

As he waits to hear back from Jesus, imagine him sitting on the hard ground of his forlorn prison cell, a confused and dejected figure, awaiting an answer to a question he never thought he would ever ask.

Yet this is the man of whom Christ said,

> *Among them that are born of women there hath not risen a greater than John the Baptist. (Matthew 11:11).*

So What Does This Teach Us?

It teaches us that doubt and discouragement can overtake the best of us. It also teaches us that there is hope for all of us, however far down the bottomless pit of discouragement we may have fallen.

In truth, the self-pity that we are tempted to wrap ourselves in like a comfort blanket is nothing more than a manifestation of the fact that we have lost sight of the Lord and have therefore become overwhelmed under the crushing stress of our circumstances.

With Jesus no longer in view, everything unravels, and we become engulfed in the paralyzing thought that we may have gotten it all horribly wrong in putting all our trust in Him.

But be of good cheer! Hear the reply of our Lord to John's candid and honest cry. Note that Jesus neither rebukes him nor expresses disappointment in him. Instead, he sent back a message of encouragement and exhortation to His beloved and faithful servant:

> *Go and shew John again those things which ye do hear and see. . . . And blessed is he, whosoever shall not be offended in me. (Matthew 11:4, 6)*

And Jesus did not stop there. After John's disciples had left to take Jesus' message back to the prison, the Lord went further in chiding those present who may have been inwardly standing in judgment over the beleaguered prophet because of his skeptical question. Jesus let them know in no uncertain terms how highly he thought of John and how precious he was to Him.

To his credit, there is no record of John ever doubting the Lord again in the remainder of his short life, and even though he was murdered soon thereafter, this last of the Old Testament prophets finished his course with joy, having kept the faith.

Let us consider this matter of becoming offended at the Lord, but from a different perspective.

In John 6, while teaching in the synagogue in Capernaum, the Lord Jesus said to His extended group of disciples,

I am the living bread which came down from heaven: if any man eat of this bread, he shall live for ever: and the bread that I will give is my flesh, which I will give for the life of the world. (John 6:51)

Some of His disciples could not understand what He was teaching them and took offense at His remarks, declaring,

This is an hard saying; who can hear it? When Jesus knew in himself that his disciples murmured at it, he said unto them, Doth this offend you? . . . From that time many of his disciples went back, and walked no more with Him. Then said Jesus unto the twelve, Will ye also go away? Then Simon Peter answered him, Lord, to whom shall we go? Thou hast the words of eternal life. (John 6:60-61, 66-68)

It is so easy to become offended at the Lord when we do not understand what He is saying to us or doing in our lives.

This scriptural account makes it clear that many of His disciples deserted Him that day, and to this day some are still deserting Him. The question Christ asks us now is, *Do you also want to go away?* If we do, He will not prevent us any more than He prevented those that day in Capernaum. But before taking that step, stop and consider that,

- Only He has the words of eternal life; all else leads to death.
- Only He is the Light, and outside of Him, there is nothing but darkness.
- Only He is the Way, and apart from Him we are lost (in every sense of the word).
- Only He is the Rock from which comes living water.
- Only He is the Good Shepherd. Without His care, the thief and his wolves are all we have to look forward to.
- Only He is the Truth; the rest are all deceivers.
- Only He is the Son of God, who loved us and gave Himself for us.

The Lord knows what you are facing. He knows because, in His omniscient love, He has designed a specific pathway of sanctification leading to glory, entirely unique to you. And His promise to you is this:

There hath no temptation taken you but such as is common to man: but God is faithful, who will not suffer you to be tempted above that ye are able; but will with the temptation also make a way to escape, that ye may be able to bear it. (1 Corinthians 10:13)

He sees you. He knows where you are. He is aware of your painful thoughts and the discouraging feelings that arise in your mind. He understands how low in doubt you have sunk at times and the questions you would ask Him if they did not seem so irreverent.

Yet He has not one word of condemnation or scolding for you, just a gentle reminder:

Blessed is he, whosoever shall not be offended in me. (Matthew 11:6)

Are you tempted to take offense at what the Lord has allowed into your life, and feel like withdrawing and turning inward, wondering whether perhaps you should "look for someone else"?

Reject Unbelief and Its Self-Pity

Return to trusting your Lord, and take the next step of faith with Him. That is all that the Lord requires of you—to trust Him enough to take the next step with Him.

He does not expect you to understand, but He does expect you to so trust Him that you say, *I do not understand,* "nevertheless not as I will, but as thou wilt" (Matthew 26:39).

The further we walk with Christ and the closer we get to Him, the more we will encounter *hard sayings* and hard circumstances. But remember that we were chosen by God and intended for glory if we do not allow ourselves to be offended at Jesus.

17

WITHOUT FAITH IT'S IMPOSSIBLE TO PLEASE GOD

(Hebrews 12:2)

We know our God to be the God of the impossible:

Ah Lord God! behold, thou hast made the heaven and the earth by thy great power and stretched out arm, and there is nothing too hard for thee. (Jeremiah 32:17)

This fact almost goes without saying, and we are entirely convinced that "with God all things are possible" (Matthew 19:26).

Yet for many of us, it is an altogether different story when the Lord asks us to act on this certainty and confidence that we profess to have in Him. Suddenly we find ourselves rationalizing, calculating, being *practical*, and generally finding every way possible to avoid putting ourselves at risk.

Still, there comes a time in the life of every true believer at which the Lord invites us to step out of the certainty and security of our boat straight onto the water—in a storm and in the dark! When that time comes, how will you respond?

Read Matthew 14:22-33.

Despite what went wrong afterward, it has to be remembered that when the moment came, *Peter alone* responded in faith. That he later sank because he moved from faith to reason was not a surprise to the Lord nor a mark against Peter.

Consider some facts about this man:

- Peter was as scared as anyone else in that boat when the silhouette of a man walking toward them appeared out on the water amid that storm.

- Peter heard the same words that the others did: "Be of good cheer; it is I; be not afraid" (Matthew 14:27).

- Peter recognized that it was Jesus but could not process the fact that He was out there, standing on the water. Yet Peter alone responded to Him with a challenge based on faith: "Lord, if it be thou, bid me come unto thee on the water" (Matthew 14:28). Something in him knew that this was indeed Jesus and that here was an unprecedented opportunity to experience Jesus' power and to please Him.

- Peter, upon receiving the invitation to come to Jesus, in an act of faith put one leg over the side, then the other, and slid down onto the churning waters beneath him, eyes no doubt riveted on Jesus who stood a little way off. Then he took the first step, then the second, his mind filled with wonder and the excitement of knowing that he was honoring his Lord with every step.

- As Peter became distracted from the Lord, his faith failed, and he sank; but he still had the confidence in Jesus to call out to Him to be saved from drowning. And the Lord responded immediately.

Jesus' next words to Peter are often taken as a rebuke, but this author believes they were instead a very precious personal moment between Jesus and His beloved Peter:

O thou of little faith, wherefore didst thou doubt? (Matthew 14:31)

In saying that Peter had "little faith," the Lord was not being critical but rather was simply stating a fact about Peter's faith at that time. It is like calling a five-year-old a *little person*. It is not a criticism but a simple statement of fact. It was no more Peter's fault that his faith was little than it is the child's fault that his stature is little. In both cases, there is growth happening, albeit slowly.

The Lord had seen Peter with his "little faith" attempt, and he partially succeeded in doing what no other man had ever done before. But doubt intervened. The Lord asked him, "Wherefore didst thou doubt?" Of course Jesus knew why, but He wanted Peter to learn for himself what it meant to trust Him.

Child of God, has the Lord called you to do the impossible? Has He asked you to step out and do what common sense says cannot be done? Are you frozen in that place between two, wanting to obey but terrified of the consequences of failure?

Like Peter, you must grasp the divinely engineered opportunity presented to you, even if it means stepping out of your boat into the impossible. Make that move even though others hold back. Obey that call even though others think you are mad.

For Peter, stepping out of that boat took more faith than walking on the water. Unbelief is paralyzing because it generates fear, and "fear hath torment [punishment]" (1 John 4:18). Fear generates the thought that something bad is going to happen to us.

Peter, with his little faith, did not give unbelief a chance to bind him in fear; instead, he got himself out of that boat.

Can you walk on water? If Jesus says come, yes, you can!

Part 2
COMFORT

"Blessed be the God and Father of our Lord Jesus Christ, the Father of mercies and God of all comfort, who comforts us in all our affliction, so that we may be able to comfort those who are in any affliction, with the comfort with which we ourselves are comforted by God."
—2 Corinthians 1:3-4

"This is my comfort in my affliction, that your promise gives me life."
—Psalm 119:50

18

PEACE

Peace I leave with you, my peace I give unto you: not as the world giveth, give I unto you. Let not your heart be troubled, neither let it be afraid.
—John 14:27

Our Lord left us peace. He gave it to us as a gift—a peace that is His peace, not the temporary, shallow, unreliable "peace" that the world offers. Indeed, not only is it His peace, but it is He in the person of the Holy Spirit who is in us to unite us with Christ. "For he is our peace" (Ephesians 2:14).

But what is this peace? It is nothing less than the consequence of being in oneness with Christ—remaining in His love, keeping our eyes on Him, trusting Him unswervingly, and walking with Him to the exclusion of all else and all others.

> *These things I have spoken unto you, that in me ye might have peace. In the world ye shall have tribulation: but be of good cheer; I have overcome the world. (John 16:33)*

In stark contrast to Christ's peace, the world is the environment that generates suffering in the lives of the saints. But our Lord has left us His Word so that we might know Him, who is our peace. And we can have absolute assurance because He has overcome the world!

Peace is the privilege of every child of God. We need not plead for it; we already have it if we would, by the Spirit, be one with Jesus in our every thought—thought by thought by thought. This is peace, a natural fruit of the Spirit:

> *But the fruit of the Spirit is . . . peace. . . . (Galatians 5:22)*

Many in the world are seeking *peace of mind*. We who are in Christ have it now:

> *For to be carnally minded is death, but to be spiritually minded is life and peace. (Romans 8:6)*

Our peace is as full, as satisfying, as never-ending, and as present as Christ is, and the promise to the one who would fully and unwaveringly trust Him is this:

> *Thou wilt keep him in perfect peace, whose mind is stayed on thee: because he trusteth in thee. (Isaiah 26:3)*

Great peace have they that love thy law, and nothing shall offend them. (Psalm 119:165)

Beware of the thief who "cometh not, but for to steal, and to kill, and to destroy." He comes to steal our peace, kill our faith, and destroy our fellowship with the Lord. We must not "give place to the devil," "lest Satan should get an advantage of us: for we are not ignorant of his devices" (Ephesians 4:27; 2 Corinthians 2:11).

And let the peace of God rule in your hearts, to which also you were called in one body; and be thankful. (Colossians 3:15)

The absence of peace in the heart of a child of God is evidence of broken fellowship with the Master, for "God is faithful, by whom ye were called unto the fellowship of his Son Jesus Christ our Lord" (1 Corinthians 1:9).

Loss of peace is therefore like an early warning system that alerts us to the fact that we have disconnected ourselves from our Lord—the Vine (John 15:5). Whenever this happens, we must instantly rectify the situation by swift repentance and return to the intimacy of fellowship (and therefore peace) that is the privilege of every saint.

The danger of a believer's heart without God's peace is that it produces a double-mindedness that is conflicted in its outlook, confused in its perspective, unstable, and susceptible to the influence of the flesh, the world, and the devil. It is a perilous place to be in.

Sadly, a child of God can grow accustomed to this lack of peace. Living without God's peace is the natural state of the unbeliever, and if our fellowship is with them and with the world, we may feel sufficiently *normal* to carry on in this way for some time. And with each spurned opportunity to repent, the heart grows harder until the Lord in love has to intervene in chastisement.

If we would but walk in the Spirit, we would know our Lord's presence with us:

And the peace of God, which passeth all understanding, shall keep your hearts and minds through Christ Jesus. (Philippians 4:7)

Lord, wherever this reader is today, in whatever circumstances, even if, like the disciples, he/she has shut himself/herself in through fear and confusion— dear Master, walk right through that closed door, and let them hear Your loving greeting: "Peace be unto you" (John 20:26).

19

UNDERSTAND THE WILL OF THE LORD

Wherefore be ye not unwise, but understanding what the will of the Lord is.
—Ephesians 5:17

There are at least two aspects to the will of God, yet the two are one. One aspect is the *permission* of God—that which the Lord allows to take place. In Romans 15:32 the apostle Paul wrote to the brethren at Rome,

. . . that I may come unto you with joy by the will of God, and may with you be refreshed.

He was hoping to be able to visit them and enjoy their fellowship but only if the Lord so desired. He was submitting himself to the permissive will of God.

The second aspect of God's will is the *purpose* of God—that which He has determined to bring to pass. For instance, every true believer is of "them who are the called according to his purpose" (Romans 8:28). And we are told that,

We have obtained an inheritance, being predestinated according to the purpose of him who worketh all things after the counsel of his own will. (Ephesians 1:11)

A child of God cannot help but walk in God's will (or purpose) as long as they do not walk in disobedience, for God's great overarching will (or purpose) is our *sanctification*:

For this is the will of God, even your sanctification. (1 Thessalonians 4:3)

Even if that person sins, the moment they repent and return to obedience they are again in the will of God, for sanctification has recommenced. But as mentioned above, the permission of God and the purpose of God are one in that He will not give us permission to do anything other than that which is in accordance with His purpose.

It is tempting from a human standpoint to focus mostly (if not exclusively) on the permissive will of God because we equate success with action, and so we are constantly seeking the Lord's permission to do this thing or that because we want to get things done for Him.

Yet the reality is that unless we start with the purpose of God and make it our one priority, the permission of God will constantly frustrate us, for if we are truly seeking after Him, He will restrict us and divert us and perhaps even isolate us from so much of what we think we should be involved in. Even the apostles were forbidden by God from doing things that seemed right and in keeping with the spread of the gospel (Acts 16:6-7).

We need to "understand what the will of the Lord is" and learn that God's purpose is paramount, and His permission is a natural outflowing from it. When we understand and accept this, we begin to think and act accordingly.

For example, we cease to be anxious.

Be anxious for nothing; but in every thing by prayer and supplication with thanksgiving let your requests be made known unto God. And the peace of God, which passeth all understanding, shall keep your hearts and minds through Christ Jesus. (Philippians 4:6-7)

We seek to have a transformed mind.

And be not conformed to this world: but be ye transformed by the renewing of your mind, that ye may prove what is that good, and acceptable, and perfect, will of God. (Romans 12:2)

We do all to the glory of God.

. . . doing the will of God from the heart. (Ephesians 6:6)

We learn to be patient, trusting God.

For ye have need of patience, that, after ye have done the will of God, ye might receive the promise. (Hebrews 10:36)

Our worldview comes into line with God's.

And the world passeth away, and the lust thereof: but he that doeth the will of God abideth for ever. (1 John 2:17)

May the constant attitude of our heart be "nevertheless not my will, but thine, be done" (Luke 22:42).

20

WEAKNESS

Have mercy upon me, O LORD; for I am weak. —Psalm 6:2

No one naturally rejoices in weakness, for weakness implies a lack of control over our destiny and points to a dependence on someone or something else. The natural man is all about personal strength and independence.

It was the prospect of that self-reliance and personal power that so appealed to Eve in the Garden:

Ye shall be as gods. (Genesis 3:5)

The carnal mind revels in the idea of being god-like—having the power to fulfil our own will when we want and how we want. The world detests a weakling and admires strength of whatever sort.

Yet contrary to the impulses of the flesh, God's will for His own is to learn total, unconditional dependence on Him. That involves a lifelong process and one which goes completely against the grain of all the carnal mind holds dear. God wants us to be made aware of just how incapable we are, by our efforts, of ever being the blameless, holy ones that He desires for us to be.

But not only does He want us to acknowledge our weakness, He wants us to even rejoice in it, for it is only in the surrendering of our will and the loss of control over our circumstances that we can ever know what it means to be Christ-like.

It is only when we see ourselves for what we are and begin to see (by contrast) the absolute perfection and power of Christ that we are finally in a position for the Lord to take forward the "good work" that He has begun in us.

Like Jacob, we must go from being self-confident, self-made schemers to limping on our staff in total reliance on God, for us to become conformed to the image of Christ.

Has the Lord begun to show you your weakness? Has he disappointed your plans, reversed your progress, allowed great failure, undone your handiwork, or stopped you utterly in your tracks? Has He removed from you your means of strength and independence and left you feeling exposed and wondering, *What now?*

It may all seem very confusing and disorienting just now, but this is a sure sign that your Lord is performing His eternal work in you.

Being confident of this very thing, that He who has begun a good work in you will complete it until the day of Jesus Christ. (Philippians 1:6)

For it is God which worketh in you both to will and to do of his good pleasure. (Philippians 2:13)

During three separate seasons of prayer and waiting, Paul earnestly sought the Lord regarding his "thorn in the flesh" (2 Corinthians 12:7). Did the Lord remove it so that Paul could get on with his life and ministry? No.

Instead, the Lord revealed something immensely more important and precious to the apostle:

My grace is sufficient for thee: for my strength is made perfect in weakness. (2 Corinthians 12:9)

Job too cried out in complaint: "God maketh my heart soft [weak]," yet we know what a glorious revelation the Lord gave Job at the end (Job 23:16). The fact is that,

He giveth power to the faint; and to them that have no might he increaseth strength. (Isaiah 40:29)

Likewise the Spirit also helpeth our infirmities [weaknesses]. . . . (Romans 8:26)

For we have not an high priest which cannot be touched with the feeling of our infirmities [weaknesses]; but was in all points tempted like as we are, yet without sin. (Hebrews 4:15)

May we, like Paul, understand the nature of the great, gracious work that is being performed in us, and be able to say, as he did,

Therefore I take pleasure in infirmities, in reproaches, in necessities, in persecutions, in distresses for Christ's sake: for when I am weak, then am I strong. (2 Corinthians 12:10)

21

TODAY

But exhort one another daily, while it is called "Today," lest any of you be hardened through the deceitfulness of sin. —Hebrews 3:13

"The deceitfulness of sin." There, in those four words, lies the great threat posed to every child of God.

Sin rarely presents itself blatantly and in its natural ugliness. Instead, it comes camouflaged, disguised in whatever form most appeals to the individual, and promises relief, deserved pleasure, an alternate path, or just a harmless distraction. But the product is always the same: death. Sin and death are two sides of the same cursed coin.

As a result of this constant threat, believers are encouraged to "exhort one another daily"—not when it comes to mind, or when it is convenient, but *daily*. Why? Because sin is deceitful, as is the adversary who would lead us into it. Sin does not fight fairly nor observe any rules. It has one intention: to dominate and bring us down into defeat (Psalm 19:13; Romans 6:14).

Think about it. If we who are Christ's do not exhort, encourage, and support each other, who will?

Now ye are the body of Christ, and members in particular [individually]. (1 Corinthians 12:27)

We and we alone are responsible for this ministry of exhortation. Yet sadly, this very day, many of the Lord's dear ones will succumb to sin because we were not there to exhort them and redirect their eyes to Jesus.

We who are "the called according to His purpose" have been given a window of opportunity to demonstrate our love and trust in Him at all times and at every stage of our ever-changing lives (Romans 8:28). That window is called *"Today,"* and the admonition is for us to stir up one another daily while we still have the opportunity, to avoid becoming hardened in our spirit by the deceitful sin that crouches at the door.

22

THE UNMOVABLE MAN

He that doeth these things shall never be moved. —Psalm 15:5

It is God's intention that we should not be moved. He would have us standing and stable, not "like a wave of the sea driven with the wind and tossed" but kept by an unshakable confidence in Him, whose "hope we have as an anchor of the soul, both sure and stedfast, and which entereth into that within the veil" (James 1:6; Hebrews 6:19).

Psalm 15 ends with the words, "He that doeth these things shall never be moved." What *things* does this refer to? In brief, chapters 15 and 16 show us *the character of the unmovable man or woman*, the one who "shall abide in thy tabernacle . . . who shall dwell in thy holy hill" (Psalm 15:1).

The unmovable man is *godly*:

- in his walk (way of thinking)
- in his works (way of living)
- in his words (way of communicating)

When everything around is pressuring him to slide ever so slightly, to drift just a bit, to shift oh so subtly, by the grace of God he is,

Stedfast, unmovable, always abounding in the work of the Lord, forasmuch as ye know that your labour is not in vain in the Lord. (1 Corinthians 15:58)

When circumstances seem to give the lie to the goodness and faithfulness of his God, he continues to "hold the beginning of [his] confidence stedfast unto the end" and remains "grounded and settled, and . . . not moved away from the hope of the gospel" (Hebrews 3:14; Colossians 1:23).

When the enemy assails him in all his fury, he knows he must,

Resist stedfast in the faith, knowing that the same afflictions are accomplished in [his] brethren that are in the world. (1 Peter 5:9)

The perfect example of the unmovable man is our Lord Jesus Christ. As we abide in Him in oneness of fellowship and submit to the sanctifying work of His Spirit within us, we, too, will be pleasing to the Father, and we,

Shall be like a tree planted by the rivers of water, that bringeth forth his fruit in his season; his leaf also shall not wither; and whatsoever he doeth shall prosper. (Psalm 1:3)

As to that prosperity, the last verse (v. 11) of Psalm 16 tells us:

Thou wilt shew me the path of life: in thy presence is fulness of joy; at thy right hand there are pleasures for evermore.

Regardless of the pressure, the temptation, and the ferocity of the assault, by the grace of our God we can be unmovable. May we therefore ever be mindful of the warning:

Ye therefore, beloved, seeing ye know these things before, beware lest ye also, being led away with the error of the wicked, fall from your own stedfastness. (2 Peter 3:17)

Thanks be to God that we can say,

I have set the LORD always before me: because he is at my right hand, I shall not be moved. (Psalm 16:8)

And this promise is true for us:

Cast thy burden upon the LORD, and he shall sustain thee: he shall never suffer the righteous to be moved. (Psalm 55:22)

"He only is my rock and my salvation: he is my defence; I shall not be moved" (Psalm 62:6). He is our God "which holdeth our soul in life, and suffereth not our feet to be moved" (Psalm 66:9).

Whatever you are facing today, dear child of God, rest in this promise:

He will not suffer thy foot to be moved: he that keepeth thee will not slumber. (Psalm 121:3)

23

HAVE YOU HEARD FROM GOD?

So then faith cometh by hearing, and hearing by the word of God.
—Romans 10:17

When we consider that "without faith it is impossible to please [God]," it becomes obvious that *faith is the foundation* upon which our walk with the Lord is based (Hebrews 11:6). But how do we acquire this faith? The answer is in our text:

"Faith comes by hearing, and hearing by the word of God."

The starting point is the Word of God. It is through His Word that we "hear" His voice. It is the very purpose of the scriptures. How unfortunate, then, that we so often come to the scriptures purely in search of answers or for material for a lesson or sermon or, worst of all, out of a sense of duty or compulsion, when our Lord so desires to communicate with us personally and specially.

When we begin to learn to come to the scriptures *expecting* to hear the "voice" of the Lord speaking to us and are satisfied with nothing less, then we will surely hear Him. And, before long, we will start to notice a depth and breadth of faith beginning to develop in us, because faith (to please God) comes by hearing (the voice of God), and that hearing comes by the Word of God.

Is it any wonder, then, that in this intense and constant spiritual battle in which we are engaged, our enemy (in alliance with the flesh and the world) seeks to keep us away from the Word of God? And if he cannot keep us from the scriptures, he tries to pervert their purpose so that we come to them for every reason other than the one for which they were intended.

Furthermore, the longer we deprive ourselves of hearing the Lord, the more our spiritual ears become dull and our heart (spirit) becomes hardened until we are virtually deaf and impervious to anything the Lord would say to us. We then come to rely on others to feed us, which is both dangerous and will never satisfy. May it be true of us that,

*The Lord G*OD *hath opened mine ear, and I was not rebellious, neither turned away back. (Isaiah 50:5)*

Only those who hunger and thirst for righteousness seek to hear the voice of God. If you know that you lack that hunger and thirst, you can have it restored by sincerely making that confession to God and asking that He renews or provides that desire, for He delights to see His own seeking after Him.

Having so petitioned the Lord, you need not wait for some great wave of emotion to sweep you up, but rather go to the scriptures and expect to hear from God—and you will, and your faith will develop, which in the exercise thereof will grow more and more until it becomes established and unshakable.

Beware of allowing the enemy to disarm you by distracting, discouraging, or deluding you from God's Word, which "quick, and powerful" and is the very Sword of the Spirit (Hebrews 4:12). The powers of spiritual darkness fear it intensely. The enemy knows that it is the source of our faith (our shield) and that which is "able to quench all the fiery darts of the wicked" (Ephesians 6:16). Therefore do not underestimate how intent Satan is on keeping us from hearing God's voice.

Our Lord Jesus desires greatly to fellowship with us in increasing intimacy. Do not be content with anything less. *Be ready to hear God speak*, and He will. Then observe with thanksgiving as His Spirit begins to develop in you a faith that pleases Him.

> *He that hath an ear, let him hear what the Spirit saith unto the churches. (Revelation 2:29)*

24

WHEN DARKNESS FALLS

> *He hath made me to dwell in darkness. . . .* —Psalm 143:3

Those who have or do presently live with the enemy we call "mental illness" understand better than any other how applicable are the words of David in this psalm:

> *For the enemy hath persecuted my soul; he hath smitten my life down to the ground; he hath made me to dwell in darkness, as those that have been long dead. Therefore is my spirit overwhelmed within me; my heart within me is desolate. (Psalm 143:3-4)*

Those who battle daily with mental health problems know in their own experiences something of what David is writing about. The sense of persecution and having been beaten down to the ground, the dwelling in darkness, the feeling of being no longer a part of life, forgotten, lonely, on the outside—like living but being dead. And of course, the natural consequence of all this is a spirit that is overwhelmed and desolate.

In another psalm, David wrote,

> *I am troubled; I am bowed down greatly; I go mourning all the day long. (Psalm 38:6)*

In Hebrew, the word *troubled* means "to pull out of proper shape; to bend; to twist; to distort." David was saying that he felt like he was being pulled apart. He was depressed and in a state of continual sorrow. This is as perfect a description of one suffering mentally as could be written.

But thank God the story does not end there! David also wrote the following:

> *The Lord upholdeth all that fall, and raiseth up all those that be bowed down. (Psalm 145:14)*

> *If I say, Surely the darkness shall cover me; even the night shall be light about me. Yea, the darkness hideth not from thee; but the night shineth as the day: the darkness and the light are both alike to thee. (Psalm 139:11-12)*

> *For thou wilt light my candle: the Lord my God will enlighten my darkness. (Psalm 18:28)*

If you are suffering from any sort of mental health issue, do not believe the satanic lie that you are of little value to God and that He has forgotten you. He has *not*; you are the focus of His attention. Nor should you believe that the oppressive darkness that overshadows you is lord of your life. It is *not*.

Jesus Christ is Lord!

And do not allow yourself to accept the idea that all hope is gone. It is *not*, for Jesus Himself is your hope, and He is a very present help in trouble.

> *The Lord raiseth them that are bowed down. (Psalm 146:8)*

He has not forsaken you.

> *Unto the upright there ariseth light in the darkness. (Psalm 112:4)*

Amid your black darkness, God's light will shine, and you will see His glory.

> *Ye are all the children of light, and the children of the day: we are not of the night, nor of darkness. (1 Thessalonians 5:5)*

Do not for a moment accept that this dark place is now your home. You are a child of light; you are not of the night nor of darkness.

. . . who hath called you out of darkness into his marvellous light. (1 Peter 2:9)

What you are experiencing is real, but how you are feeling at this time is just that—a *feeling*. It is not who you are, for you have been called out of darkness into His marvellous light.

. . . the Father of lights, with whom is no variableness, neither shadow of turning. (James 1:17)

Our God dispels darkness with His light. He is also a constant and unchangeable light in our lives. There is no sunset with God.

God is light, and in him is no darkness at all. (1 John 1:5)

He Himself is light. The darkness you face is not of Him nor from Him. Do not believe the lie that God is punishing you. Even though He has allowed this in your life at this time, be sure that the light of His presence is still there with you, even if you struggle to see it right now.

Arise, shine; for thy light is come, and the glory of the Lord is risen upon thee. (Isaiah 60:1)

25

THE WORTH OF WAITING

Behold, as the eyes of servants look unto the hand of their masters, and as the eyes of a maiden unto the hand of her mistress; so our eyes wait upon the Lord our God, until that he have mercy upon us. —Psalm 123:2

Waiting upon God in hope is not suspending life until the Lord arrives, nor is it a subtle way of admitting defeat, nor yet of putting an issue out of our minds, but is instead the *vital element* in our transformation into the image of Christ (as well as part of God's battle strategy for us).

Waiting upon God necessitates reliance upon Him and involves the Word of God and prayer, which always replenishes faith and strength.

This discipline of waiting upon the Lord is so important that much time is spent in scripture either teaching this principle or demonstrating it in the lives of the faithful. We must grasp the significance that God places on this issue. If we fail to understand this, or worse, fail to live in the light of this truth, we cut ourselves off from God's blessing here, doom ourselves to defeat at the hands of the enemy, and deprive ourselves of future blessings and rewards.

In short, if we are not prepared to wait on God, we will never know Him in this life as He intended and never please Him as He desires.

Waiting On God Is Common to All True Believers

Every righteous man and woman recorded in scripture had their life and character *shaped on the wheel of patience*, perfectly crafted by the Potter's hand. Hence, we are admonished to,

> *Take, my brethren, the prophets, who have spoken in the name of the Lord, for an example of suffering affliction, and of patience. Behold, we count them happy which endure. Ye have heard of the patience of Job and have seen the end [intended by] the Lord; that the Lord is very compassionate, and of tender mercy. (James 5:10-11)*

The Flesh Detests the Idea of Waiting On God

Oh, how the flesh revolts against the very notion of having to wait! And especially having to wait upon God. We do not mind *working*—our naturally independent (carnal) self wants to be doing something, going somewhere, achieving some goal—but the whole idea of having the matter taken out of our hands fills us with dread. Being required to rely on God without knowing His specific intentions or His time frame is maddening and frankly intolerable to the carnal mind.

When we are feeling weak and need strength, we want it *now*. Yet we are told,

> *Wait on the LORD: be of good courage, and he shall strengthen thine heart: wait, I say, on the LORD. (Psalm 27:14)*

When we have been wronged, we want justice *without delay*. But we read,

> *Say not thou, I will recompense evil; but wait on the LORD, and he shall save thee. (Proverbs 20:22)*

When we encounter fiery trials, we want deliverance *instantly*. But what saith the scriptures?

> *But let patience have her perfect work, that ye may be perfect and entire, wanting nothing. (James 1:4)*

It is no surprise, then, that many within "Christianity" are so enamored with anyone who promises a quick fix, a shortcut to success, or a way to jump the queue and get what we want *now*. Whether this is offered by way of a special prayer, the use of some verse of scripture plucked out of its scriptural context, a "new" revelation of the Spirit, or just by way of the tried and tested invitation, "Send me your money, and I'll send you the cure," it is astonishing the lengths we will go to avoid having to wait on God.

Why?

- Because the carnal man's focus is on a goal, not on God.
- Because his mindset is a product of the world and is therefore constantly in a hurry.
- Because waiting on God would deprive such a person of being able to claim the glory for the achievement.
- Because it makes no sense to be waiting when one could resort to more pragmatic means.
- Because it is not exciting, visible, or in any way attractive.
- Above all, and at the root of it all, because *we simply do not believe God.*

What God Wants Us to Understand About Waiting On Him

But what does "the God of patience and consolation" say to us about waiting upon Him (Romans 15:5)?

He would have us *meditate upon His Word:*

For whatsoever things were written [in earlier times] were written for our learning, that we through patience and comfort of the scriptures might have hope. (Romans 15:4)

He would have us *observe the lives of the faithful:*

That ye be not slothful, but followers of them who through faith and patience inherit the promises. (Hebrews 6:12)

Above all, He would have us *look to Jesus:*

Wherefore seeing we also are compassed about with so great a cloud of witnesses, let us lay aside every weight, and the sin which doth so easily beset us, and let us run with patience the race that is set before us, looking unto Jesus the author and finisher of our faith. (Hebrews 12:1-2)

God's Response to Waiting Upon Him

How does God respond to the one who, in reliance, waits confidently upon Him even as the battle of their personal circumstances rages on?

He giveth power to the faint; and to them that have no might he increaseth strength. Even the youths shall faint and be weary, and the young men shall utterly fall: but they that wait upon the LORD shall renew their strength; they shall mount up with wings as eagles; they shall run, and not be weary; and they shall walk, and not faint. (Isaiah 40:29-31)

To wait upon God is *not an inactive pause* but is the most exciting, thrilling, active part of our lives, for it is the time when we know beyond any doubt that we are walking with God—not before Him or behind Him but in step with Him—walking in the Spirit. It is a time of such intimate fellowship with Him and with a sense of being part of the Master's grand design.

What could be more satisfying than knowing that with every waiting minute that goes by, we are bringing pleasure and joy to the heart of our Lord as we continue to trust and worship Him in our waiting? Not waiting for an answer, not even so much as waiting *on* Him, but rather waiting *with* him.

Is it not time for us to repent and do the first works? Should not God's priorities determine ours? It is only as we separate ourselves from the culture of the world, the desires of the flesh, and the lies of the devil that we will begin to comprehend the glory of the ways of God and hence the worth of waiting.

For ye have need of patience, that, after ye have done the will of God, ye might receive the promise. (Hebrews 10:36)

26

THE LORD IS IN THE DETAILS

All this, said David, the LORD made me understand in writing by his hand upon me, even all the works of this pattern. —1 Chronicles 28:19

There is a pattern to all that God does in the lives of His children—a deliberate, predestined, detailed plan. For the most part, we cannot perceive this pattern in our lives, and we need to walk by faith, believing that,

. . . all things work together for good to them that love God, to them who are the called according to his purpose. (Romans 8:28)

What we need to consider, though, is that all that God does is done perfectly and in intricate, exact detail, and it is there that we often find ourselves diverging from God's plans.

We rejoice in the big picture or product of God's plans, but we often struggle with the details of it because we fail to realize that the Lord is in the details. It is in the nitty-gritty—the working out of our Lord's purposes in us—that we see why He refers to our lives as a *walk* . . . step by step by step. Each step is a detail in the plan of conformation into the image of Christ. Step by step, thought by thought, choice by choice, decision by decision, the plan takes shape to the glory of God.

David said that the Lord had given him understanding of all the details of the plans for the temple "in writing by His hand upon [him]" (1 Chronicles 28:19). Likewise, we too have been made to understand the details (or steps) through the Spirit illuminating His Word to our hearts. He would have us follow the instruction that Mary gave to the servants:

Whatsoever he saith unto you, do it. (John 2:5)

If those details happen to be difficult, do it! If they are painful and seem harsh, do it! If they lead to obscurity and loneliness, do it! If they mean monotonous, daily repetition of apparently inconsequential tasks, do it! If they mean being ostracized, do it! If they lead your life in a totally unexpected and undesirable direction, do it!

Do it, and keep doing it! Follow every step of God's plan because the Lord is in the details.

27
ALL OR NOTHING

I beseech you therefore, brethren, by the mercies of God, that ye present your bodies a living sacrifice, holy, acceptable unto God, which is your reasonable service. —Romans 12:1

The unfathomable mercies of God in calling and choosing us should logically compel us to give Him our all. Nothing short of full, genuine, joyful surrender of our lives will suffice.

Yet, though this choice seems so clear, so many of us fail to see that this verse is directed personally to each one of us, and so we conclude that it is probably safe (and even acceptable) to carry on living on our own terms, giving God what we think we can spare.

Amaziah provides a salient and sobering lesson about what happens when we think we can serve God as it suits us. His life is summed up in the following verse:

*He did that which was right in the sight of the L*ORD*, but not with a perfect heart. (2 Chronicles 25:2)*

In brief, Amaziah did many good and commendable things, but his heart (his spirit) was never fully the Lord's—he never obeyed God with his *whole heart.* On the face of it (at least for a while), there was little or nothing to indicate that Amaziah was anything other than what he appeared to be: a godly king of Judah. But,

*The L*ORD *seeth not as man seeth; for man looketh on the outward appearance, but the L*ORD *looketh on the heart. (1 Samuel 16:7)*

Inevitably, Amaziah's true nature began to come to the fore. First, he chose to ignore the fact that many of the people were still involved in occultic activities—*he closed his eyes to the truth.*

Then, after his great victory over the Edomites, he brought back some of their idols and began worshipping them. His heart filled with pride, and he provoked a fight with the king of Israel, who warned him to desist. But "Amaziah would not hear" (see 2 Chronicles 25:15-20). *He closed his ears.* He engaged Israel in a fight, lost badly, and was further humiliated by having part of the wall of Jerusalem torn down, having all the gold and silver plundered, and having to watch as the king of Israel departed with many of his people in tow as prisoners.

Not only had he lost the nation's wealth, but he had also lost his reputation and the respect of the people. His life ended with him on the run, and he finally met the same fate as his father: assassinated by his own servants. How could it have come to this? Because he never sought after God with his whole heart.

The parallel account in 2 Kings says,

*He did that which was right in the sight of the L*ORD*, yet not like David his father [ancestor]. (2 Kings 14:3)*

His heart was not like David's, of whom God had said,

I have found David the son of Jesse, a man after mine own heart, who shall fulfil all my will. (Acts 13:22)

Half-hearted surrender is a compromise that God will never accept. Either Christ is Lord, or He is not. No partial submission or semi-surrender will ever be countenanced by God, nor will He engage in any negotiation or deal. With God, it is *all or nothing.*

Amaziah's life again proves that "[a] double-minded man is unstable in all his ways" (James 1:8). By contrast, the psalmist said,

With my whole heart have I sought thee: O let me not wander from thy commandments. (Psalm 119:10)

The Lord Jesus Himself said,

He that loveth father or mother more than me is not worthy of me: and he that loveth son or daughter more than me is not worthy of me. And he that taketh not his cross, and followeth after me, is not worthy of me. He that findeth his life shall lose it: and he that loseth his life for my sake shall find it. (Matthew 10:37-39)

Nothing but our all can ever truly please God. And is He not worth it?

Worthy is the Lamb that was slain to receive power, and riches, and wisdom, and strength, and honour, and glory, and blessing. . . . (Revelation 5:12)

. . . and our all.

28

STAND STILL

Wherefore take unto you the whole armour of God, that ye may be able to withstand in the evil day, and having done all, to stand.
—Ephesians 6:13

At times in our pilgrimage through this life, we encounter genuinely hard, perplexing situations to which there seem to be no clear answers and, crucially, no certain end. The longer it persists (or the more often it occurs) the more deflated and faint we tend to become, to the point where discouragement sets in, and we begin to feel trapped and defeated.

What are we to do when we have prayed in faith, and nothing happens? When we have waited in hope, and there is no change? When we have done the right thing and yet face the same crushing situation day after day?

Where do you go when no one seems to have a satisfactory answer, and often the more we seek the help of man the more we regret ever having tried? Time passes and the world moves on, but our battle for survival in the quicksand of our circumstances continues.

A Lesson from Biblical History

When in sheer terror and unbelief, the people of Israel lashed out at Moses (and God) as they saw the approaching Egyptian army. The scriptures record,

And Moses said unto the people, Fear ye not, stand still, and see the salvation of the LORD, which he will show to you today. (Exodus 14:13)

And what a deliverance it was!

"And Having Done All, to Stand"

When "the evil day" comes, all we can do and all we *should* do is refuse to fear and stand still in faith! That may not sound like much of a plan, and it certainly does not seem logical, but it is what we *must* do if we are to see the Lord's deliverance.

The reality when facing severe or protracted trials is that it is out of our control and beyond our understanding. In addition, we have no idea of its future intensity or duration, or whether there will be a sudden and miraculous deliverance. We simply do not know, and there is nothing we can do for ourselves. There is only this: "Fear ye not, stand still" (Exodus 14:13)!

We may feel it is time for something to happen, yet God says, "Fear not. Stand still!"

We may feel like the Lord has forgotten us, but He hasn't. He says, "Fear not. Stand still!"

We may feel that we cannot fight for one more minute, but still, God says, "Fear not. Stand still!"

We may feel (and may look) silly for not trying to take matters into our own hands and forcing a result, and yet God says, "Fear not. Stand still!"

I wait for the LORD, my soul doth wait, and in his word do I hope. My soul waiteth for the LORD more than they that watch for the morning: I say, more than they that watch for the morning. (Psalm 130:5-6)

Amid the heat, noise, or loneliness of our battles,

Let us hold fast the profession of our faith without wavering; (for he is faithful that promised). (Hebrews 10:23)

Stand still, beloved, and see the salvation of the Lord.

29

KNOWING THE WILL OF GOD

Wherefore be ye not unwise, but understanding what the will of the Lord is.
—Ephesians 5:17

The general will of God is encapsulated in three sets of commandments: the Ten Commandments (Exodus 20:2-17), the Great Commandment (Matthew 22:37-40), and the New Commandment (John 13:34). A summary of these might be stated as "love God and love others, but especially the brethren" (see 2 Corinthians 8:5).

Regarding the specific will of God—that is, that which pertains to the individual circumstances of our lives—*the Lord Himself* is the answer to this quest, for to know the Lord is to know His will, since He promised to manifest Himself to those who will love Him and keep His Word (John 14:21).

It is futile to expect the Lord to reveal to us moment by moment every detail of our lives, for He will not. One reason is that, as He explained,

My thoughts are not your thoughts, neither are your ways my ways, saith the Lord. *For as the heavens are higher than the earth, so are my ways higher than your ways, and my thoughts than your thoughts. (Isaiah 55:8-9)*

Another reason has to do with our conformation to the image of Christ. Experiences like not knowing what to do next, living with apparently unanswered prayer, or looking back over our lives and not being able to make sense of the many twists and turns, all bring us to one point: *Will I still believe God?* If the answer is no, then the sanctifying process stops. If yes, then we are becoming more and more like our Lord, even if we cannot see it in ourselves.

In John chapter 6, after Jesus had made a particular statement to the people, it is recorded that some said, "This is an hard saying; who can hear it?" (John 6:60). It further states that "From that time many of his disciples went back, and walked no more with him" (John 6:66).

These had come to the end of their quest to know the will of God; it had reached the point of being too hard for them to keep going.

Then said Jesus unto the twelve, Will ye also go away? Then Simon Peter answered him, Lord, to whom shall we go? thou hast the words of eternal life. And we believe and are sure that thou art that Christ, the Son of the living God. (John 6:67-69)

Peter and his companions may not have fully understood Christ's earlier statement either, but they were not letting go of *Him*. They knew that all answers lie with Him and that they were standing in the very presence of the will and Word of God.

Has trusting God become too hard? Have you grown weary as you have waited for direction, explanation, or rescue? Are you planning to go back and walk with Jesus no more? Or will you, like Peter, acknowledge that in Christ you have already found the answer to every question, the solution to every problem, the explanation for every riddle, and the source of all that is good?

Many books have been written about knowing the will of God, and many a sermon preached. Yet so many are perplexed and have become distracted and indeed discouraged because we feel that we don't know what the will of the Lord is for us personally.

Yet, as we have seen, the will of God is bound up in the knowledge of Christ, hence Paul's declaration in which he summarized the intent of his life:

> *That I may know him, and the power of his resurrection, and the fellowship of his sufferings, being made conformable unto his death.* *(Philippians 3:10)*

Beware of the loss of your first love. God never instructed us to love His will; He commanded us to love *Him*. The wonderful reality is that in loving Him and staying our minds on Him, we, in the Spirit, will be effortlessly walking in the specific will of God.

The Lord has no interest in hiding His will from us. Quite the contrary! He wants us to know His will, but not independently of Him—not purely to satisfy our curiosity. Rather, He desires to lead us step by step as we walk with Him by faith.

30

EARS TO HEAR
(PART 1)

He that hath ears to hear, let him hear. —**Matthew 11:15**

If the Lord has granted you ears to hear, you *must* hear. Spiritual hearing is a unique gift of grace from God, and the recipient must see it as such.

To ignore or quench this gift is to hold the Spirit of grace in contempt (Hebrews 10:29).

This gift of spiritual hearing is also the source of our faith, which itself is our shield in the great spiritual battle in which we are engaged.

So then faith cometh by hearing and hearing by the word of God. (Romans 10:17)

There is no other way to receive faith but by hearing God, and the only way to hear God is by His Word; whether we hear Him as we read it or later as He, in His own unique way, illuminates what we have read.

It is possible to read the Word of God and never hear from God, not because He does not speak but because we do not have ears to hear. Simply having knowledge of the scriptures does not guarantee hearing. "Knowledge puffeth up" but "the knowledge of the holy is understanding" (1 Corinthians 8:1; Proverbs 9:10). If we love God with all our heart, long for His fellowship, and are desperate to hear from Him, He will surely manifest Himself to us and grant us understanding.

How often do we go to the Word of God with good intentions but not in the Spirit? The result is that, though we may find some degree of encouragement, we lose out on the more profound, more personal messages that the Lord desired to communicate to us. We are so busy listening to our own thoughts that it never occurs to us to listen to His.

Alternatively, we are sometimes guilty of going to the scriptures with an agenda, whatever that might be, and we may well succeed in this quest . . . but at what cost? We may acquire facts but no fellowship of the Spirit. We may prove a point and miss out on an appointment with God. We may come away feeling educated but not edified. Why?

Because while the brain may have taken in its fill, the spirit is malnourished because we robbed ourselves of the opportunity to hear with spiritual ears. We cannot approach God or His Word in the way that the world approaches the acquisition of knowledge, for we are not of the world:

Now we have received, not the spirit of the world, but the spirit which is of God; that we might know the things that are freely given to us of God. (1 Corinthians 2:12)

To hear from God, we must be in actual, present, personal oneness of fellowship with Christ in spirit. Not merely intellectually but in spirit and in truth. The test is to stop and ask oneself, *To whom am I listening this instant?* If the answer is not Jesus, then we need to immediately start listening to Him with our spirit.

The Lord has His own way of speaking to us when we are spiritually attuned. As we fellowship with Him in our spirit, He is able to communicate Spirit to spirit and show us profound truths in a moment of time.

Speak, Lord; for thy servant heareth. (1 Samuel 3:9)

31

EARS TO HEAR
(PART 2)

Today if ye will hear his voice, harden not your hearts. . . . —Hebrews 3:15

What does it mean to harden one's heart?

It is the act of making one's spirit deaf to the voice of the Spirit of God and is referred to in scripture in various ways: quenching the Spirit (1 Thessalonians 5:19), stopping the ears (Zechariah 7:11), turning the back (Jeremiah 2:27), hearing but not doing (Ezekiel 33:32; James 1:22), and shrugging the shoulders and stiffening the neck (Nehemiah 9:29).

The intent is always the same—to make oneself impervious to the voice of God so as to be free to follow another voice espousing a more attractive way.

Yet how can this be if,

He is our God; and we are the people of his pasture, and the sheep of his hand[?] (Psalm 95:7)

Sheep who do not follow the voice of the shepherd quickly become isolated or lost and often end up as prey. Again, why would we who know the goodness of the Good Shepherd not follow His voice at all times?

Generally speaking, as long as all is well and the weather is set fair for us, we are more than happy to hear the Lord, for we see the benefits to ourselves. However, when things change and we find ourselves not just in grave trials but unexpectedly so, we quickly begin accommodating a different voice— the voice of doubt and eventually that of desperation, and we soon arrive at *Massah* (test) and *Meribah* (quarrel) as we begin to quarrel with and test the Lord, wondering (at least in our hearts),

Is the LORD among us, or not? (Exodus 17:7)

During trials, when we stop listening to the voice of God, we begin listening to the thoughts of doubt, which lead to despair, then disdain for God, and finally to disobedience. At this point, only a divine act of grace can get our attention sufficiently to provide us with the opportunity to repent and return to the place of faith and attentiveness.

Psalm 95:11 says,

Unto whom I sware in my wrath that they should not enter into my rest.

There is no rest or peace for the one who closes his ears and turns his back in annoyance at God. Yet the scriptures tell us,

Thou wilt keep him in perfect peace, whose mind is stayed on thee: because he trusteth in thee. (Isaiah 26:3)

Beloved,

Let us therefore fear, lest, a promise being left us of entering into his rest, any of you should seem to come short of it. For unto us was the gospel preached, as well as unto them: but the word preached did not profit them, not being mixed with faith in them that heard it. (Hebrews 4:1-2)

How often have we heard a brother or sister say, "Oh that the Lord would speak to me." Yet the issue is never that God does not speak but rather that we do not listen.

God has spoken and recorded it in His Word. God is still speaking to the hearts of all who are His, using His Word to direct us in the various circumstances of our lives. But a hardened heart of unbelief will never hear His voice, for it is occupied with the din of quarrelling and complaints against God. It is too busy finding a more palatable alternative to the restrictive, narrow, often difficult path along which our Master leads us.

So that brings us back to *today:*

Today if ye will hear his voice, harden not your hearts. . . . (Hebrews 3:15)

He that hath an ear, let him hear what the Spirit saith unto the churches. (Revelation 2:29)

32

GOD KNOWS

Behold, the eye of the Lord is upon them that fear him, upon them that hope in his mercy. —**Psalm 33:18**

God knows." We have all uttered these words at some point in our lives—sometimes in exasperation, sometimes in sad resignation, and sometimes simply in an attempt to bolster ourselves up to hold on. But if we truly consider those two words, a tremendous truth emerges before us, a truth that can change the entire way in which we perceive ourselves and our circumstances.

God's eye is on you. There is *nothing* about you that He cannot see. There is nowhere that you can go that obscures His vision. There is nothing that can enter your life that blinds Him from His focus on you. You can never disappear from His sight because His eye is upon you.

> *And she called the name of the Lord that spake unto her, Thou God seest me. (Genesis 16:13)*

God *sees* you.

> *The Lord is far from the wicked: but he heareth the prayer of the righteous. (Proverbs 15:29)*

When you pray, when you call out to God, when you cry out to Him, He hears you every time. There is *never* a time when He does not hear. No circumstance, no act, no development, no failing on your part can ever prevent Him from hearing you.

> *O thou that hearest prayer, unto thee shall all flesh come. (Psalm 65:2)*

God *hears* you.

> *Thou knowest my downsitting and mine uprising, thou understandest my thought afar off. Thou compassest my path and my lying down, and art acquainted with all my ways. For there is not a word in my tongue, but, lo, O Lord, thou knowest it altogether. (Psalm 139:2-4)*

This shows that God both knows and understands you. Not as part of a group but you, *yourself.* He knows your thoughts, your hopes, your doubts, and your deepest, most hidden fears. He knows everything about you, and He understands you infinitely more than you (or anyone else) ever could.

God *knows* and *understands* you.

Thou hast beset me behind and before, and laid thine hand upon me. (Psalm 139:5)

God has surrounded you with His love and claimed you as His own. You won't get lost in your circumstances nor can anyone or anything approach you without His permission. He has determined every event that is to take place in your life. You are not aimlessly drifting along as you trust in a faraway God who has left you to figure things out for yourself. No! He is with you in every way, to your eternal benefit and His glory.

My times are in thy hand. (Psalm 31:15)

God *has His hand upon* you.

Yes, God knows. This moment, let His Spirit infuse you with this great, life-changing truth. Permit your faith in God to awaken in the light of this reality. Allow yourself to finally rest in the security and comfort of the fact that God knows.

33

GRACE TO STAND STILL

And Moses said unto the people, Fear ye not, stand still, and see the salvation of the Lord. —**Exodus 14:13**

Most of us perceive the walk of the believer as a walk of activity—doing things for God. But the reality is that for the majority of the time, the Lord requires us to simply stand still.

Stand Still to Fellowship

We must stand still if we are to know what it means to be continuously fellowshipping with Christ.

We are never more deaf to the voice of the Spirit than when we are busy running to and fro, trying to achieve things for God. It is like trying to pass on a message to someone as they drive by at a hundred miles per hour. We are so busy with our "purpose-driven" lives that we become increasingly unable to hear "the author and finisher of our faith" (Hebrews 12:2). Instead, we settle for old manna, secondhand or filtered instructions, or just making it up as we go along.

Stand Still to Fight

We must stand still if we are to be overcomers amid all that is taking place around us and in us.

There is a most vicious spiritual battle on Earth: Satan and his demonic spirits, assaulting the children of God because we have God's Spirit in us. In this great spiritual war, we must learn to stand still if we are to be equipped with "the whole armour of God" (Ephesians 6:11). This "armour of light" is put on, not in pieces but as one whole, for this is nothing less than "put[ting] on the Lord Jesus Christ"—i.e., abiding in Him so that He can be our complete defense and that we "may be able to withstand in the evil day, and having done all, to stand" (Romans 13:12, 14; Ephesians 6:13).

Stand Still to Move Forward

As contradictory as this may sound, it is an immutable principle of God that the only way to receive His direction is by first standing still.

When in Numbers chapter 9 a new challenge presents itself involving some of the men of the children of Israel, Moses did not jump to a hasty conclusion so that they could move on. Instead, he said to them,

> **Stand still, that I may hear what the LORD will command concerning you. (Numbers 9:8)**

This man, who had on his shoulders the responsibility for the entire nation of Israel, and who, therefore, had every excuse to rush, chose instead to stand still and seek the face of God for the way forward in that situation— and of course, God led him.

Caution

Let us be careful, though, not to confuse the need to stand still with idleness, fear, or cold-heartedness, all of which are the products of the flesh and/or induced by the enemy. And it doesn't take much to know the difference. We need only ask the Lord; He will show us the true state of our heart.

Remember, too, that regarding anything the Lord may want us to do, there is a time for waiting and a time for responding. Moses told the men who came to him in Numbers 9 to stand still while he sought God, but once the Lord had spoken, so did Moses.

The key to doing anything for the Lord is bound up in the lesson of the pillars of fire and cloud in the book of Exodus, both of which represented the presence of the Lord with Israel. When they stood still Israel stood still, and when they moved on so did Israel.

We do not have these visible pillars today, nor the *Urim* and *Thummim*, or many obvious miraculous signs, but we have something infinitely better: we have the Spirit of the living God indwelling each of us who are His.

It surprises us when, in retrospect, we realize that most of our walk with the Lord involved standing still. And this standing still, this rest before God as the world around us rushes from one thing to another, is no slight or easy discipline. It requires His grace moment by moment, but it comes with such tremendous promises:

> *Those that wait upon the L*ORD*, they shall inherit the earth. (Psalm 37:9)*

> *Wait on the L*ORD*, and he shall save thee. (Proverbs 20:22)*

> *But they that wait upon the L*ORD *shall renew their strength; they shall mount up with wings as eagles; they shall run, and not be weary; and they shall walk, and not faint. (Isaiah 40:31)*

> *Be still, and know that I am God. (Psalm 46:10)*

May our gracious God open our eyes to the importance of standing still before Him, so that He can speak to us, and through us influence others to do the same by the peace that is evident in our lives.

> *Wait on the L*ORD*: be of good courage, and he shall strengthen thine heart: wait, I say, on the L*ORD*. (Psalm 27:14)*

Part 3

EXHORT

*"Until I come, devote yourself to the public reading of
Scripture, to exhortation, to teaching."
—1 Timothy 4:13*

*"He has told you, O man, what is good; and what does the
Lord require of you but to do justice, and to love kindness,
and to walk humbly with your God?"
—Micah 6:8*

34

NOT ONE THING

Not one thing hath failed of all the good things which the LORD your God spake; . . all are come to pass unto you, and not one thing hath failed thereof.
—Joshua 23:14

At the end of Joshua's extraordinary life, he called all the leaders and elders of the nation of Israel to him and, as Moses had done before him, recited in their hearing all the great goodness and faithfulness of God who had brought them to the land in which they now dwelt. He summed it all up in one memorable phrase: "Not one thing hath failed of all the good things which the LORD your God spake concerning you."

What a remarkable testimony given by this old warrior before he died! After decades with Moses and then as the leader himself, Joshua could say that there was *not one thing* in which God had failed.

There are few things more uplifting than listening to the testimonies of elderly brothers and sisters in Christ. As they speak of their sojourn here, their experiences differ widely, but their testimonies all have the same theme: *the faithfulness of God.*

Since Eden, Satan has tried to undermine faith in God. Yet those who have trusted in the Lord throughout their lives have, without exception, declared Him utterly faithful. After innumerable trials, hardships, and bewilderments, their universal conclusion and testimony to the next generation is,

> *Know therefore that the LORD thy God, he is God, the faithful God, which keepeth covenant and mercy with them that love him and keep his commandments to a thousand generations. (Deuteronomy 7:9)*

Jeremiah declared it thus:

> *Remembering mine affliction and my misery, the wormwood and the gall. My soul hath them still in remembrance, and is humbled in me. This I recall to my mind, therefore have I hope. It is of the LORD's mercies that we are not consumed, because his compassions fail not. They are new every morning: great is thy faithfulness. (Lamentations 3:19-23)*

He said, in effect, that despite all his suffering (and no doubt many unanswered questions), he could say without any doubt, "great is thy faithfulness."

Sometimes amid the crush of life, we can lose perspective; that is to say, we can lose sight of the fact that,

God, that cannot lie, promised. . . . [or that] God is faithful, by whom ye were called unto the fellowship of his Son Jesus Christ our Lord. (Titus 1:2, 1 Corinthians 1:9)

It is an indisputable fact that whatever severe trials we find ourselves in, God is faithful. Indeed, *great* is His faithfulness. Let us stand firm in the name of He who is faithful and true: our Lord Jesus Christ.

Beloved, consider this: as you look back over your life, can you genuinely name one thing in which God was unfaithful? Not one thing! There is not one thing in which He has not been true to His "exceeding great and precious promises" (2 Peter 1:4).

Cast not away therefore your confidence, which hath great recompence of reward. For ye have need of patience, that, after ye have done the will of God, ye might receive the promise. For yet a little while, and he that shall come will come, and will not tarry. Now the just shall live by faith: but if any man draw back, my soul shall have no pleasure in him. But we are not of them who draw back unto perdition; but of them that believe to the saving of the soul. (Hebrews 10:35-39)

May we be strengthened by the reality of His faithfulness and walk on with Him by faith.

35

ONE THING HAVE I DESIRED

One thing have I desired of the LORD, that will I seek after; that I may dwell in the house of the LORD all the days of my life, to behold the beauty of the LORD, and to enquire in his temple. —**Psalm 27:4**

Our ambitions are like a window into our true selves and speak volumes about who we really are, because our ambitions originate in the heart. That which we long for most manifests itself in our priorities, passions, and focus. We cannot hide our true selves for very long, for the scriptures teach us that our very words reveal our hearts:

> *A good man out of the good treasure of his heart bringeth forth that which is good; and an evil man out of the evil treasure of his heart bringeth forth that which is evil: for of the abundance of the heart his mouth speaketh. (Luke 6:45)*

Indeed, it is impossible to hide who we are, for,

> *Ye shall know them by their fruits. Do men gather grapes of thorns, or figs of thistles? Even so every good tree bringeth forth good fruit; but a corrupt tree bringeth forth evil fruit. A good tree cannot bring forth evil fruit, neither can a corrupt tree bring forth good fruit. (Matthew 7:16-18)*

Both our words and our works reveal the ambitions of our hearts.

Reading Psalm 27, one is struck by the unmistakable ambition of David. We know that he petitioned the Lord for and about many things over the years of his life, but there was *one thing* that he requested above all else, a plea that revealed his deepest desire and greatest longing, which was to be as close to God as possible and to be granted the privilege of uninterrupted worship.

One can sense in his words a single-minded love, an unbreakable bond, a blindness and deafness to all distractions, an abandonment of all for this *one thing*, and an insatiable hunger and thirst for God. David had a heart for God.

For some who profess to be believers, Christ is but a means to an end. But in truth, He is both the means *and* the end for righteousness to those who truly trust in Him. God's children do not serve Him *for* something, they serve him *because of* something, and that something is His unfathomable love manifested in the Lord Jesus Christ—their hearts' goal and prize and unrivaled joy is Christ.

David had one desire, one goal, one aim, and that was to fellowship with and worship his God. He said in another psalm,

> *My heart is fixed, O God, my heart is fixed: I will sing and give praise. (Psalm 57:7)*

He had a heart for God alone.

Paul's ambition was,

> *That I may know him, and the power of his resurrection, and the fellowship of his sufferings, being made conformable unto his death. (Philippians 3:10)*

Is it true of us that,

> *For to me to live is Christ, and to die is gain[?] (Philippians 1:21)*

Does our heart cry out to God,

I stretch forth my hands unto thee: my soul thirsteth after thee, as a thirsty land[?] (Psalm 143:6)

Are we so desperate for God that we would say,

As the hart panteth after the water brooks, so panteth my soul after thee, O God[?] (Psalm 42:1)

Amid all that is happening around us and to us, when we lift up our eyes from it all, do we see Jesus only (Matthew 17:8)? Can we genuinely say,

Whom have I in heaven but thee? and there is none upon earth that I desire beside thee. (Psalm 73:25)

Which way do our ambitions lie? What *one thing* do we desire above all else? Do we truly have a heart for God? The answer will reveal who we are and shape our destiny.

36

ONE THING LACKING

Then Jesus beholding him loved him, and said unto him, One thing thou lackest. . . . —Mark 10:21

This man did not come to Jesus by accident or out of casual curiosity. He came because he wanted something, and he believed that if anyone could give it to him, Jesus could. He came prepared—he ran, he knelt, he flattered. He felt that this was his chance, and he was going to seize it!

So what was it that this man so desired?

He already had more wealth than most people could even dream of. He seemed in good health and well-informed. What more could a man wish for who already had everything he wanted in life? The answer: more life—in fact, never-ending life. He had, as it were, pulled down his barns and built greater ones. Now, it was time for this businessman to secure the ultimate deal. He sought to have eternal life—but, ironically, in the end, he was unwilling to pay the price required.

The Lord Jesus gave him three opportunities to stop and recognize his spiritual poverty:

1. First, Jesus exposed his flattery for the empty talk that it was: "There is none good but one, that is, God" (Mark 10:18). That seemed to have had no impact on him.
2. Second, He pointed him to the commandments (which no one until Jesus had ever kept perfectly), naming six that had to do with our interaction with others. The rich man claimed to have kept not some but all of them, and not once but consistently from his youth up.
3. Finally, the Lord told him to give away his wealth and to follow Him. That was the end of the conversation; the deal was off! He had come to Jesus excited and expectant but went away "sad . . . and . . . grieved" (Mark 10:22).

In three steps, the Lord had shown this man his heart. Now there was no more pretense, no more flattery or boasting, just a man whose heart was demonstrated to be "deceitful above all things, and desperately wicked" (Jeremiah 17:9). And though he left the presence of Christ saddened and grieving, he did not leave repentant. Why?

Because he had lacked *one thing*: a heart that was truly seeking God, for he already had his god—mammon (wealth)—and that left no room for Christ.

> *No servant can serve two masters: for either he will hate the one, and love the other; or else he will hold to the one, and despise the other. Ye cannot serve God and mammon. (Luke 16:13)*

The man thought that he could simply add eternal life to his other riches without realizing that the Man before whom he knelt was the Way to God, the Truth of God, and the Life eternal, which could only be accessed by entering through Him who is the Door.

The rich man never discovered this because he had no intention whatsoever of parting with his current, familiar, tangible god—his wealth. It was all well and good for Christ to promise "treasure in heaven," but this man was not about to lose his treasure on earth for any number of promises (Mark 10:21).

The reality is, though, that this man was by no means a one-off. Many have decided to reject Christ and keep their god(s) and therefore could never have the salvation they knew they needed. Others, having "tasted of the heavenly gift, and . . . made partakers of the Holy Ghost" (Hebrews 6:4) reach a stage at which they decide that spiritual adultery is not so much a sin as an acceptable compromise to have,

the best of both worlds - Christ + my god(s)

If one is in any doubt of the reality of the danger of such thinking, we need look no further than the following scripture:

I know thy works, and thy labour, and thy patience, and how thou canst not bear them which are evil: and thou hast tried them which say they are apostles, and are not, and hast found them liars: And hast borne, and hast patience, and for my name's sake hast laboured, and hast not fainted. Nevertheless I have somewhat against thee, because thou hast left thy first love. (Revelation 2:2-4)

Left to go where? To love another god, even if that is not how they would have characterized it at the time. They had not divorced the Lord and said goodbye; they had simply left, gradually, almost imperceptibly. They did not see themselves as idolaters (we never do); they had simply become attracted to someone or something else and rationalized their attachment to it/them, all the while continuing to carry out all the duties of a faithful spouse.

One striking statement in the account in Mark 10 is that "Jesus beholding him loved him" (Mark 10:21). Even though he knew that this man would reject Him, He loved him. And not just that man, but the lawyers, the Pharisees, the scribes, the Romans, the crowd who shouted, "Crucify him!", and the soldiers who drove the nails into His hands and feet. Why? Because God is love, and His Son manifested this.

Just as Jesus could see the heart of this rich man, He can see ours:

Neither is there any creature that is not manifest in his sight: but all things are naked and opened unto the eyes of him with whom we have to do. (Hebrews 4:13)

It behooves us, therefore, to examine ourselves in the presence of the Holy Spirit and see whether, despite our past faithfulness and present commitment, there is one thing lacking, and if so, to,

Remember therefore from whence thou art fallen, and repent, and do the first works. (Revelation 2:5)

37

ONE THING IS NEEDFUL

But one thing is needful: and Mary hath chosen that good part, which shall not be taken away from her. —Luke 10:42

Making choices is a fundamental part of life. It is also undoubtedly true that, in the end, we are the sum of those choices. Every day, every minute, indeed in every thought we are making choices. Some are very obviously made, while others are such that we are almost unaware of having made them.

A choice is a decision, and decisions are the paths along which we travel in this life. These paths, in turn, determine our eventual destination (*decisions determine destination*). It is evident, therefore, how critical it is that we make the right choices every time we are required to do so.

Having decided to invite Jesus into her house, Martha's next choice was one of natural hospitality: to begin to prepare the best possible meal for the most important of guests. She expected that, as Jesus was left to relax (possibly in the company of Lazarus), her sister, Mary, would quickly join her, and together they would prepare the best feast at their disposal. However, Mary never arrived at the kitchen but remained with Jesus, as she had been since He entered the house.

Annoyed at her sister's apparent lack of common sense, Martha appealed directly to Jesus, obliquely scolding Him, too, for not having sent Mary away to assist in the preparations. She exclaimed,

> *Lord, dost thou not care that my sister hath left me to serve alone? Bid her therefore that she help me. (Luke 10:40)*

Was Martha acting carnally, caring more about customs and formalities than she did about the Lord? Certainly not! Martha loved Jesus just as much as Mary and Lazarus did, and the Lord loved her (John 11:5). No, this was the exasperation of a godly (if temporarily misdirected) woman who felt that the most obviously important thing for her and her sister to be doing just then was making sure that the Master felt welcomed (in the traditional Eastern way) by the preparation of the best meal possible. This was not an unreasonable request on her part, but there was a better path available.

Mary's choice was that she,

> *. . . sat at Jesus' feet, and heard his word. (Luke 10:39)*

The Lord was sharing truth, as was ever the case when He spoke, and Mary was determined to miss not a word of it.

Was she not aware that Jesus may well have been hungry, or that the normal thing for her to do was to be preparing the guest's meal? Of course she did. But for her only *one thing* mattered: sitting at the Master's feet and drinking in His eternal words.

The Lord's reply to Martha's complaint is typically gentle but profoundly instructive:

> *Martha, Martha, thou art careful and troubled about many things: But one thing is needful: and Mary hath chosen that good part, which shall not be taken away from her. (Luke 10:41-42)*

Martha was worried and troubled about many things, but Mary had chosen the *one thing* that was needed, the Lord describing it as "that good part" and promising that it would not be taken from her—i.e., the Word of God, which she was absorbing into her heart, could never be snatched away or lost.

We, too, are daily confronted with many decisions (every motion of our minds involves a decision), and it is extremely easy to be worried and troubled about many things—legitimate things, urgent things, burdensome things, even things concerning others . . . things that are real and pressing. But our Lord would have us choose "that good part," for only *one thing* is needful, and that is full attention to Him.

Few of us rejoice to sit at the feet of Jesus and hear His Word. We feel that we should be busy doing "great things" (or at least something) for God. We believe that the measure of our success as believers is the extent to which we can point to what we have been able to accomplish for the Lord. We acclaim the men and women who have tangible results to show for their time invested in the work of the Lord. We love to read their biographies and hear their testimonies, and we can't get enough of the "How to" books containing "tried and proven" steps to success in ministry or other work for God.

Yet for all the achievements of men, and despite all that they may have to offer, "that good part" can only be had from the Lord Himself, "for one is your Master, even Christ" (Matthew 23:10). Everything for the child of God comes back to Jesus Christ. There may be many useful things in which we could get very involved, but only *one thing* is needful, and that is absolute, unrivalled devotion and attention to our Lord, to the extent that, in comparison, nothing else matters.

Again, the kingdom of heaven is like unto a merchant man, seeking goodly pearls: who, when he had found one pearl of great price, went and sold all that he had, and bought it. (Matthew 13:45-46)

This merchant knew that he had found the only thing that mattered to him, and he was willing to give up everything else to possess it.

Paul did the same:

But what things were gain to me, those I counted loss for Christ. Yea doubtless, and I count all things but loss for the excellency of the knowledge of Christ Jesus my Lord: for whom I have suffered the loss of all things, and do count them but dung, that I may win Christ. (Philippians 3:7-8)

Is Jesus Christ our one passion, for whom we would gladly give up everything and everyone else? Is He our one focus? Is oneness with Him our one goal? Is hearing His voice our one desire? Is learning from Him our one plan and becoming like Him our one ambition?

We are full of care and troubled about many things, but only *one thing* is needful. Let us choose that "good part."

38

ONE THING I DO

Brethren, I count not myself to have apprehended: but this one thing I do, forgetting those things which are behind, and reaching forth unto those things which are before, I press toward the mark for the prize of the high calling of God in Christ Jesus. —**Philippians 3:13-14**

As we grow closer to Christ, we begin to recognize the heinous nature of our sin, and we are greatly tempted to collapse into despair and become consumed with a morbid reliving of the events of our failure. But we must not. Instead, we are to repent of any known sin, and having done so, arise and go forward, seeking to walk worthy of our heavenly calling in Christ Jesus.

Self-loathing and dwelling upon our miserable failures may appear, on the face of it, to be a commendable response to sin, but it is a trap engineered by the flesh and exploited by the devil. He knows that for as long as we are preoccupied with ourselves, we have ceased "looking unto Jesus" and started walking in the flesh, in which "dwelleth no good thing" (Hebrews 12:2; Romans 7:18).

Yet for some of us, the idea of moving on with the Lord after repentance seems like letting ourselves off far too lightly. We feel within ourselves that we are worthy of some greater punishment or at least a painful, constant reminder that we must never fall like that again. We also feel a need to demonstrate to the Lord that we are sincere in our repentance by inflicting on ourselves our version of censure and permanently viewing ourselves as unique failures.

But the truth is that Jesus Christ has paid the appallingly horrible price for the redemption of humanity. There was no "getting off lightly." In addition, God knows our hearts. He knows repentance when He sees it and does not need our assistance or seal of confirmation.

The truth about our failures is that they demonstrate that we have not yet "apprehended"—i.e., we are not yet fully in the image of Christ. There is, therefore, but *one thing* that we must do in response to past failures:

> *But this one thing I do, forgetting those things which are behind, and reaching forth unto those things which are before, I press toward the mark for the prize of the high calling of God in Christ Jesus. (Philippians 3:13-14)*

We must fix our minds on Christ and on what He has ahead for us with Him. We must forget what is behind us and be consumed with what is ahead of us, and thus pursue the prize: God's upward call in Christ Jesus.

> *Know ye not that they which run in a race run all, but one receiveth the prize? So run, that ye may obtain. (1 Corinthians 9:24)*

As simplistic as this may sound, it is this *one thing* that will make the difference between finishing our course as overcomers or being overcome and suffering great spiritual loss.

As we walk with the Lord, His direction of travel is always *forward*. Indeed, our Lord stated unequivocally,

> *No man, having put his hand to the plough, and looking back, is fit for the kingdom of God. (Luke 9:62)*

See the example of our Savior who prophetically spoke through Isaiah:

> *For the LORD GOD will help me; therefore shall I not be confounded: therefore have I set my face like a flint, and I know that I shall not be ashamed. (Isaiah 50:7)*

We, too, must set our faces like a flint, undeterred, unflinchingly pressing toward the finish line at any cost, following the example of our Lord,

> *. . . who for the joy that was set before Him endured. (Hebrews 12:2)*

Let us do this *one thing:* having left the past where it belongs, let us press toward the mark with all our heart and soul and might until we reach the prize.

39

ONE THING I KNOW

He answered and said, Whether he be a sinner or no, I know not: one thing I know, that, whereas I was blind, now I see. —John 9:25

The carnal, unbelieving mind will always reject the things of God, even when their authenticity and reality are staring them in the face, and indeed there is nothing that one can do to persuade a person who is resolute in their opposition to God. If it ended there, it would be tragic but limited to that individual, but a wider, more serious problem occurs when that stout unbeliever tries to force their unbelief onto someone who does believe in God.

Such was the case with this blind man to whom Jesus had given sight. Over and over the religious leaders questioned him in vain, hoping to be able to latch onto something, anything that might discredit Jesus. Their furious insistence and outright attempts to intimidate this man is the standard operating procedure to this day: pressure to say or do "the right thing" with jobs, careers, relationships, and more at stake. It behooves us, therefore, to learn a lesson from this simple man standing before the leaders of his nation.

Having been questioned both by his neighbors and then the Pharisees, the man kept repeating the plain facts of what had occurred. But not receiving the answer they wanted, the Pharisees questioned his parents and then the man again, this time in no way hiding their bias and brazenly instructing the man as to what he should say, namely that Jesus was a sinner. The man's response was as factual as it was infuriating for the religious leaders:

Whether he be a sinner or no, I know not: one thing I know, that, whereas I was blind, now I see. (John 9:25)

This formerly blind man knew *one thing* for a fact: that he was blind but that Jesus gave him sight. And he clung to that one thing!

Eventually the Pharisees cast the man out of the synagogue—a most serious sentence in Jewish New Testament times. Jesus later found him and revealed to him that He, the One who had given him sight, was indeed the Christ, and the man believed in Him immediately.

The spiritually blind Pharisees had sought to force this man to deny what he knew to be true, and you, dear believer, will undoubtedly face similar pressure at some point in your life, living in this world that is increasingly anti-Christ.

So how should we deal with such attempts to not only make us doubt what we know, but further, to force us to conform to the beliefs of another? The answer is this: "One thing I know, that, whereas I was blind, now I see."

He who came to bring "recovering of sight to the blind" opened our eyes one day and manifested Himself to us (Luke 4:18). No committee, no organization, no government, no relative, friend or foe . . . *no one* can change that fact.

Our eyes have been opened, and no one can close them again. So beloved, all we need do is stand with the knowledge of the truth in our heart: "and having done all, to stand" (Ephesians 6:13). Hold firmly to the one thing which, when everything else is stripped away, still stands. The one thing which, when the waves cease crashing and the storm be overpast, still remains unmoved and unmovable.

There may be many questions to which we have no answers, and we may not be able to provide the sort of "proof" that unbelievers may demand. But if we can cling to that *one thing* that we know—the reality and love of God—we may be cast out of a thousand synagogues. But Jesus will always make His presence and love known to us.

Men may shriek and threaten in all manner of ways, but nothing that anyone says or does can ever change what Jesus did for us and who He is to us. Hold to that *one thing* at any cost. Let your unceasing testimony be,

[I] was lost, and [am] found. . . . whereas I was blind, now I see. (Luke 15:24; John 9:25)

Blessed are they which are persecuted for righteousness' sake: for theirs is the kingdom of heaven. Blessed are ye, when men shall revile you, and persecute you, and shall say all manner of evil against you falsely, for my sake. Rejoice, and be exceeding glad: for great is your reward in heaven: for so persecuted they the prophets which were before you. (Matthew 5:10-12)

40

BE NOT IGNORANT OF THIS ONE THING

But, beloved, be not ignorant of this one thing, that one day is with the Lord as a thousand years, and a thousand years as one day. —2 Peter 3:8

All our experiences in this life have at least one thing in common: they are all subject to time. Our life became a prisoner to time ever since the sin of Eden, and subsequently, the repeated reality has been, "and he died." We are born, we live, and we die.

Because of our mortality, time has become interwoven into everything that we do and are. We have had to accept that life and time are inseparable.

Not so with God. He is variously described in scripture as,

The eternal God. (Deuteronomy 33:27)
The eternal Spirit. (Hebrews 9:14)
The everlasting God. (Isaiah 40:28)
Everlasting Father. (Isaiah 9:6)
[He] whose goings forth are from of old, from everlasting. (Micah 5:2)
[He who is] from everlasting to everlasting. (Psalm 90:2)

This is not a concept that the human mind can truly grasp. We push our thinking out as far as we can but always reach a point where we can go no further, for even our imaginations have limits.

Yet God "left not himself without witness" in that whether mankind searches with a microscope or telescope, he comes to the same inescapable conclusion: that there is no end to what is around us (Acts 14:17). In other words, God has given us a small but unmistakable insight into His eternal nature as seen in creation.

The unbeliever in his blindness may not recognize this, but the saint of God must not be forgetful of this *one thing:* that our God is *eternal.* He it is who says, "Before me there was no God formed, neither shall there be after me" (Isaiah 43:10). He alone "inhabiteth eternity" (Isaiah 57:15).

We are so sorely tempted to be conformed to this world because it is what we see and hear and experience all around us. Yet the Lord has told us that,

To every thing there is a season, and a time to every purpose under the heaven. (Ecclesiastes 3:1)

That teaches us that all we experience "under heaven" is seasonal, not eternal. There is the temporary (seasonal), and there is the eternal. We who are Christ's must, for a while, live in the temporary but at all times be focused on the eternal, for this is our destiny and the very nature of our God.

This helps explain why Paul wrote to those who were suffering intensely,

For which cause we faint not; but though our outward man perish, yet the inward man is renewed day by day. For our light affliction, which is but for a moment, worketh for us a far more exceeding and eternal weight of glory; While we look not at the things which are seen, but at the things which are not seen: for the things which are seen are temporal; but the things which are not seen are eternal. (2 Corinthians 4:16-18)

Solomon wrote,

He hath made every thing beautiful in his time: also he hath set the world in their heart, so that no man can find out the work that God maketh from the beginning to the end. (Ecclesiastes 3:11)

As the seasons of life swiftly come and go—a time to do this and a time to do that—the child of God (usually in retrospect) sees the hand of the eternal God making beautiful so much that is anything but. Not that He necessarily provides answers or changes circumstances, but rather He transforms us over time into the image of Christ, He who is altogether "beautiful and glorious" (Isaiah 4:2).

Peter wrote the words of our text to believers under severe trials and persecution. To compound their suffering, scoffers were taunting them about the perceived delay in the coming of the Lord to rescue them. These blind aggravators were, in effect, repeating the words of their ancient counterparts in the Psalms: "Where is thy God?" (Psalm 42:3). To the ignorant, mortal time is paramount; they measure everything by it and weigh every decision on it.

Peter wanted his brethren to remember this *one thing:* unlike us, God is eternal—eternal in His nature and therefore in His plans and work. A day, a thousand years, a quadrillion years is all the present to He who is from everlasting to everlasting, He who is both outside of time and in control of it. And *you* are the center of His focus and His love.

Know this, that all that we experience in this "moment" we call our lifetime is minutely engineered and controlled by the eternal God who has an eternal plan for you, His eternal child, and He is "not slack" concerning *any* of His promises (2 Peter 3:9).

He operates on a level infinitely beyond us; hence He informs us,

My thoughts are not your thoughts, neither are your ways my ways. (Isaiah 55:8)

We, therefore, need to be constantly "looking unto Jesus," which changes our focus from the temporary to the eternal, and from the often ugly to the always beautiful (Hebrews 12:2).

Beloved, be not ignorant of this one thing. . . . (2 Peter 3:8)

41

ENLISTED

Thou therefore endure hardness, as a good soldier of Jesus Christ. No man that warreth entangleth himself with the affairs of this life; that he may please him who hath chosen him to be a soldier. —2 Timothy 2:3-4

Have you ever considered the significance of being called by God to be a soldier in this spiritual war? It is a reality that is not often addressed or explained. Yet it is to this very thing that we are called, indeed, enlisted:

Fight the good fight of faith, lay hold on eternal life, whereunto thou art also called. (1 Timothy 6:12)

As such, we are commanded to live a life of spiritual discipline:

No man that warreth entangleth himself with the affairs of this life; that he may please him who hath chosen him to be a soldier. (2 Timothy 2:4)

Peter pleaded with the brethren thus:

Dearly beloved, I beseech you as strangers and pilgrims, abstain from fleshly lusts, which war against the soul. (1 Peter 2:11)

Concerning the battle itself, scripture tells us that,

We wrestle not against flesh and blood, but against principalities, against powers, against the rulers of the darkness of this world, against spiritual wickedness in high places. (Ephesians 6:12)

Furthermore, it tells us that,

The weapons of our warfare are not carnal, but mighty through God to the pulling down of strong holds. (2 Corinthians 10:4)

Concerning this battle Paul said, "So fight I, not as one that beateth the air," and near the end of his life he could say, "I have fought a good fight, I have finished my course, I have kept the faith" (1 Corinthians 9:26; 2 Timothy 4:7).

We battle on three fronts—the flesh, the world, and the devil—yet all three are of one nature, namely rebellion against God. Of these three, the one that directly involves us is the flesh, and the battle in this arena can be fierce,

> *But I see another law in my members, warring against the law of my mind, and bringing me into captivity to the law of sin which is in my members. (Romans 7:23)*

We need to see each other as Paul saw Archippus, whom he described as "our fellowsoldier"—our comrade in arms seeking to stand firm and please God (Philemon 1:2).

The battlefield is no place for equivocation or distraction. We must be sober and vigilant, having put on Christ who is the whole armor of God. And we must be prepared to "endure hardness, as a good soldier of Jesus Christ" (2 Timothy 2:3), as we follow in our Master's footsteps, knowing that, at the end, when we have overcome,

> *There is laid up for me a crown of righteousness, which the Lord, the righteous judge, shall give me at that day: and not to me only, but unto all them also that love his appearing. (2 Timothy 4:8)*

May the Lord illuminate our understanding and stir our hearts as we see ourselves as *the enlisted.*

> *Fight the good fight of faith, lay hold on eternal life, whereunto thou art also called. (1 Timothy 6:12)*

42

LONELINESS

I watch, and am as a sparrow alone upon the house top. —Psalm 102:7

Loneliness is one of the most difficult experiences a human being can endure. The fact that the Lord stated during creation, "It is not good that the man should be alone," demonstrates how unnatural it is for us to remain in that state, which can lead to mental, physical, and even spiritual damage in some circumstances (Genesis 2:18).

Most of us do not choose to be alone. It is often thrust upon us, sometimes in the most tragic of circumstances—the death of a loved one, a divorce, expulsion from family (perhaps for loving Christ), physical or mental afflictions that necessitate living apart from others, even loneliness in a local church into which you cannot fit despite longing for fellowship. There are many reasons why someone may find themselves in a solitary condition.

The Lord Jesus knew what it meant to be truly lonely. Growing up as a young man and knowing who He was must have been incredibly lonely. Despite having godly parents and eventually disciples who were with Him day and night throughout His ministry period, He would still have been acutely aware that there was no one like Him. He had no human equal with whom He could fellowship.

Often scriptures record that He would be alone praying (see Matthew 14:23). Even when He was being thronged by the multitudes, in one sense, He was still very much alone. Yet in this, our Lord taught us a great truth. Jesus said,

> *And yet if I judge, my judgment is true: for I am not alone, but I and the Father that sent me. (John 8:16)*

> *And he that sent me is with me: the Father hath not left me alone; for I do always those things that please him. (John 8:29)*

> *Behold, the hour cometh, yea, is now come, that ye shall be scattered, every man to his own, and shall leave me alone: and yet I am not alone, because the Father is with me. (John 16:32)*

Amid His human loneliness, He was never truly alone because He had the Father with Him. Nor are we ever truly alone because we have Christ *with* us—not just watching over us but personally indwelling us by His Spirit. What comforting grace flows from this blessed reality!

When we, by faith, grasp the all-encompassing provision in the fact of the presence of Christ in us, we are never the same again. Yes, we may still experience human loneliness at times, but that is outshone by the reality of the presence of the Son of God Himself.

Yet we must beware. As with any other trial with which we have to deal, "Sin lieth at the door. And unto thee shall be his desire, and thou shalt rule over him" (Genesis 4:7). In the case of loneliness, that sin can take the form of self-pity, bitterness, apathy, selfishness, defensiveness, withdrawal, and more.

But when we recognize that our circumstances, which are beyond our control, are completely in His control, our outlook starts to change. When we begin to see that we did not *end up* where we are but rather that, in His rich wisdom and knowledge, in His unsearchable judgements, and in His ways which are past finding out (Romans 11:33), He has brought us to this place, the eyes of our understanding become open.

Jeremiah said, "I sat alone because of thy hand" (Jeremiah 15:17). Has the Lord placed His hand on you and positioned you in the place where you can know "the fellowship of His sufferings" through loneliness (Philippians 3:10)? Then know that, far from being forsaken, His hand is upon you. Like the writer of Psalm 102, you too may feel like,

> *. . . a pelican of the wilderness . . . an owl of the desert . . . a sparrow alone upon the house top. (Psalm 102:6-7)*

But *you are not alone!*

> *I will never leave thee, nor forsake thee. (Hebrews 13:5)*

> *I am with you always, even unto the end of the world. (Matthew 28:20)*

43

TUNNELS

He hath fenced up my way that I cannot pass, and he hath set darkness in my paths. —Job 19:8

Darkness is not something we associate with God. Yet we "strangers and pilgrims" encounter times that can only be described as especially dark (1 Peter 2:11).

Sometimes these experiences are so protracted that they seem endless, and we begin to feel like we are trapped within its gloom. It is at these times that we begin to experience what could be called *carnal* tunnel syndrome—a spiritual condition in which we begin to doubt the fundamentals about God, things of which we were previously convinced, such as the love of God, His presence with us, His guiding hand upon our lives, His shielding grace, etc.

But it is when it feels like the walls of our trial are closing in on us that a certain panic begins to grip us as we strain our eyes in the darkness, hoping to glimpse even the slightest speck of light at the end of our tunnel . . . but there is none. It is then that our thinking starts to truly change.

Job said,

> *He hath fenced up my way that I cannot pass, and he hath set darkness in my paths. (Job 19:8)*

Jeremiah cried out,

> *He hath led me, and brought me into darkness, but not into light. (Lamentations 3:2)*

Heman wrote,

Thou hast laid me in the lowest pit, in darkness, in the deeps. (Psalm 88:6)

These and many more knew the *tunnel* and the *despair* that can result from it. Are you in the tunnel right now, dear brother, dear sister? Do you feel like these men quoted above speak for the way you feel? It may well be no consolation to you whatsoever, but please know that you are where so many of God's choicest have been over the centuries and, indeed, where some are this very moment.

At such times when we feel claustrophobic and fearful of the overwhelming darkness, what does the Lord expect of us? What would He have us do? Simply put, He would have us stand firmly in the dark on "those things which are most surely believed among us" in the light, for the Light is still with us (Luke 1:1):

For thou art my lamp, O LORD: and the LORD will lighten my darkness. (2 Samuel 22:29)

The LORD is my light and my salvation; whom shall I fear? (Psalm 27:1)

For with thee is the fountain of life: in thy light shall we see light. (Psalm 36:9)

Rather than trying to see the light at the end of the tunnel, see the Light who is right here and now, and say, like Micah,

When I fall, I shall arise; when I sit in darkness, the LORD shall be a light unto me. (Micah 7:8)

This then is the message which we have heard of him, and declare unto you, that God is light, and in him is no darkness at all. (1 John 1:5)

If we therefore begin looking to our God (following the example of our Lord Jesus Christ), we will have changed our focus from darkness to light. Jesus Himself said,

I am the light of the world: he that followeth me shall not walk in darkness, but shall have the light of life. (John 8:12)

Did He mean that we would never find ourselves in dark, hard places? No. But He wanted us to know that even there, He is our Light.

The enemy would have us believe that God cannot operate in our darkness. That He somehow has to wait outside to see whether or not we will make it out. *That is a lie!* David tells us that nothing impedes the progress of Almighty God:

He made darkness his secret place; his pavilion round about him were dark waters and thick clouds of the skies. (Psalm 18:11)

Not even darkness can stop our God!

If I say, Surely the darkness shall cover me; even the night shall be light about me. Yea, the darkness hideth not from thee; but the night shineth as the day: the darkness and the light are both alike to thee. (Psalm 139:11-12)

Light is sown for the righteous, and gladness for the upright in heart. (Psalm 97:11)

Beloved, do not allow yourself to fall prey to the unbelief that stalks in the dark like a hungry predator. Remember, the Light Himself is with you (indeed, in you) and will shine in you until the tunnel suddenly disappears.

Who is among you that feareth the LORD, that obeyeth the voice of his servant, that walketh in darkness, and hath no light? let him trust in the name of the LORD, and stay upon his God. (Isaiah 50:10)

44

GRACE IS NOW

Brethren, the grace of our Lord Jesus Christ be with your spirit. Amen.
—Galatians 6:18

The grace of our Lord Jesus Christ is his enabling us to be like Himself in our spirit and therefore in our character.

We all need the grace of God. Without it, we are doomed to failure, defeat, and sin, especially in times of trial and affliction. But there is something about this grace that we must understand.

The grace of God is not for the past (for that is done and gone), nor is it for the future (for that is yet to come). The grace of our Lord is for *now*—the present, this very moment in which we are living. It is here and now that we experience God's grace, for it is here and now that we need it.

We are prone to look back and wonder about past situations and circumstances and become cast down because we see inadequacy and failure on our part. We tend to do the same regarding the future, ruminating and even predicting what might or might not be, and as a result, we begin to feel overwhelmed by what we believe lies before us.

But why do we find ourselves cast down about the past or overwhelmed about the future? It is because we have projected ourselves into a time frame that does not possess the grace of God, for it is either past or yet to come. In this position, we are extremely vulnerable to the enemy's lies and deception, and we can reach a place where we lose our intimate fellowship with Jesus because our minds are elsewhere—in a place where Christ's grace is not.

We are instructed to "walk in the Spirit" and to abide in Christ (the two are the same; Galatians 5:16; John 15:4). This can only happen in the present, in the moment of now. Christ Himself is our grace, and as we abide in Him, we abide in grace. It is "the grace of our Lord Jesus Christ." The Lord's grace upon our spirit.

That is the grace we need. That is the sweet and intimate fellowship that we can have with our Lord. That is where Christ does the impossible for us. Grace sufficient for the present moment. No more but no less. The gift of grace. Amazing grace! Abundant grace! Exceeding grace! True grace!

The grace of our Lord Jesus Christ be with you all. Amen. (2 Thessalonians 3:18)

45

OUR SECRET PLACE WITH GOD

Thou shalt hide them in the secret of thy presence from the pride of man: thou shalt keep them secretly in a pavilion from the strife of tongues. —**Psalm 31:20**

The Lord has a special, secret place of intimacy reserved only for those who will draw nigh to Him. James gives more detail:

Draw nigh to God, and he will draw nigh to you. Cleanse your hands, ye sinners; and purify your hearts, ye double minded. (James 4:8)

We see here that entrance into this secret place is conditional upon us having clean hands (our actions) and a pure heart (our thoughts). We see it again in Psalm 24:

Who shall ascend into the hill of the LORD? Or who shall stand in his holy place? He that hath clean hands, and a pure heart. (Psalm 24:3-4)

The Lord will never coerce us into this fellowship. We must come willingly and gladly into His secret place. Indeed, we must yearn for it above all else.

David knew that place. He wrote,

I have set the LORD always before me: because he is at my right hand, I shall not be moved. . . . Thou wilt shew me the path of life: in thy presence is fulness of joy; at thy right hand there are pleasures for evermore. (Psalm 16:8, 11)

Because David so desired the Lord, he was established and enjoyed the fullness of joy that so many forfeit due to an unwillingness to pay the price of drawing nigh to God. And there is a price, but one that is "not worthy to be compared with the glory which shall be revealed in us" when finally "this corruptible shall have put on incorruption, and this mortal shall have put on immortality" (Romans 8:18; 1 Corinthians 15:54). Can there be anywhere safer or more comforting?

In that sweet place of intimacy, our Lord shades us in the tent of His glorious presence from the heat of the unrelenting attacks upon us. Here,

He maketh [us] to lie down in green pastures: he leadeth [us] beside the still waters. He restoreth [our] soul: he leadeth [us] in the paths of righteousness for his name's sake. (Psalm 23:2-3)

For in the time of trouble he shall hide me in his pavilion: in the secret of his tabernacle shall he hide me; he shall set me up upon a rock. (Psalm 27:5)

He that dwelleth in the secret place of the most High shall abide under the shadow of the Almighty. (Psalm 91:1)

But further, there is also the secret place of His secrets. This is a place where our Lord goes further and manifests Himself to those who have proven themselves obedient and faithful and therefore worthy of a deeper, fuller knowledge of Him.

He that hath my commandments, and keepeth them, he it is that loveth me: and he that loveth me shall be loved of my Father, and I will love him, and will manifest myself to him. (John 14:21)

The secret of the LORD is with them that fear him; and he will shew them his covenant. (Psalm 25:14)

. . . his secret is with the righteous. (Proverbs 3:32)

For the love of Christ, for the glory of God, for our eternal good and that of many others, let us ensure that we are both in God's secret place and in His place of secrets,

Until the day dawn, and the day star arise in [our] hearts. (2 Peter 1:19)

46
WILLING AND ABLE
(PART 1)

Watch and pray, that ye enter not into temptation: the spirit indeed is willing, but the flesh is weak. —Matthew 26:41

We need to have a willing spirit in our relationship with Christ. There is nothing we can do about the flesh—it is weak, sinful, and passing away. But we do have control of our spirit (1 Corinthians 14:32) and must constantly submit it to the lordship of Christ (2 Corinthians 10:5).

This is of paramount importance especially when we are enduring suffering because it is then that we can faint spiritually and fall prey to the enemy's lies. To "faint" is to draw back from the Lord in unbelief.

The scriptures are full of exhortations not to faint:

- We must not faint in *prayer*.

  And he spake a parable unto them to this end, that men ought always to pray, and not to faint. (Luke 18:1)

- We must not faint when *suffering*.

  Therefore seeing we have this ministry, as we have received mercy, we faint not; . . . by manifestation of the truth commending ourselves to every man's conscience in the sight of God. . . . For which cause we faint not; but though our outward man perish, yet the inward man is renewed day by day. (2 Corinthians 4:1-2, 16)

- We must not faint when *our brethren are suffering*.

  Wherefore I desire that ye faint not at my tribulations for you, which is your glory. (Ephesians 3:13)

- We must not faint when *doing right*.

  And let us not be weary in well doing: for in due season we shall reap, if we faint not. (Galatians 6:9; also 2 Thessalonians 3:13)

God always responds to a willing heart:

If any man will do his will, he shall know of the doctrine, whether it be of God, or whether I speak of myself. (John 7:17)

. . . and He is ever urging us to come closer:

Draw nigh to God, and he will draw nigh to you. (James 4:8)

David prayed,

Restore unto me the joy of thy salvation; and uphold me with thy [willing] spirit. (Psalm 51:12)

May this also be the constant prayer of our hearts: that we may be ever willing, even if in ourselves we are not able.

The first step is for us to examine ourselves in the presence of the Spirit of God to see whether we are truly willing to follow Christ however and wherever He may lead our lives. Remember, it is better to be willing and fall short than not to be willing at all (Proverbs 24:16).

May we be truly willing to walk with our Lord, in green pastures and parched, in still waters and storms, in success and failure. And may our hearts hunger and thirst for righteousness, for in our willingness He will make us able.

47

WILLING AND ABLE
(PART 2)

But Jesus answered and said, Ye know not what ye ask. Are ye able to drink of the cup that I shall drink of, and to be baptized with the baptism that I am baptized with? They say unto him, We are able.
—Matthew 20:22

James and John meant well. They wanted to be as close as possible to Jesus. Yet their request to sit one on the right hand and the other on the left hand of Jesus in His kingdom was a request based on ignorance. They had no idea what would be involved in fulfilling their request.

Some of us have made similar requests of the Lord—well intentioned and no doubt zealous but in similar ignorance. The reality is that there is a cost involved in being close to Jesus, one that we should consider soberly and sincerely if we mean what we say.

Jesus asked those disciples, "Are ye able to drink of the cup that I shall drink of, and to be baptized with the baptism that I am baptized with?" Their immediate answer was, "We are able." Think about those three words for a few moments in the context of what Jesus had asked them.

Christ had lived a perfect life before His Father and was now about to lay down that life as the Lamb of God, taking away the sin of the world. In the course of that act, God,

> *. . . made him to be sin for us, who knew no sin; that we might be made the righteousness of God in him. (2 Corinthians 5:21)*

That was the cup that Jesus was about to drink and the baptism that He was about to be baptized with.

Were James and John able to endure lifelong suffering in obedience to Christ? Would they stand firm and never waver, whatever the circumstances? Could it be said of them by the Father that He was well-pleased in them? Could they truly drink the cup of pain and undertake the baptism of the refiner's fire?

We too must come to a place of grasping the humbling reality that though we may be willing, *we are not able*—not in ourselves or by our power or ability, regardless of our zeal.

If we are ever to truly draw close to Jesus, we must first make the calculation and acknowledge the high price that must be paid (Luke 14:25-33). The Lord is asking for everything, bar none. He wants to be acknowledged as absolute Lord or not at all.

We are not able. But God is.

> *And God is able to make all grace abound toward you; that ye, always having all sufficiency in all things, may abound to every good work. (2 Corinthians 9:8)*

He is able in everything, at every time, so we can have every sufficiency for every situation. "The Lord is able to make [you] stand," for it is He "that is of power to establish you" (Romans 14:4; 16:25).

Have you a willing heart? That is pleasing to the Lord. But know and remember that only Christ's strength can enable us to be who we should be. The willing heart that sees the limitations and weaknesses of the flesh has come to the place that the apostle Paul reached of which he wrote,

> *And he said unto me, My grace is sufficient for thee: for my strength is made perfect in weakness. Most gladly therefore will I rather glory in my infirmities, that the power of Christ may rest upon me. Therefore I take pleasure in infirmities, in reproaches, in necessities, in persecutions, in distresses for Christ's sake: for when I am weak, then am I strong. (2 Corinthians 12:9-10)*

48

WHEN TO STOP BELIEVING GOD

The faith of Abraham. . . . who against hope believed in hope. . . .
—Romans 4:16, 18

When should we stop believing God?

- When the answer doesn't come *in time*?
- When circumstances become worse?
- When we are ridiculed for believing?
- When we feel like God won't answer?
- When we feel unworthy?
- When it begins to cost too much?
- When we become discouraged?

It is neither difficult nor uncommon to have a *feeling* of trust in God, especially when things are going our way. But what happens when that trust is severely tested in some way? Should we continue to trust Him . . . or not?

Faith that pleases God is based on only one thing: the nature of God as expressed in Jesus Christ. In other words, the only faith that is worth anything in the sight of God is that which believes in who He *is*, not what He can give us. This is why God gave His name as I Am (*Yahweh*).

God simply *is* . . .

- One in His uniqueness
- Eternal in His existence
- Love in His character
- Light in His manifestation
- Perfect in His works
- Omniscient in His knowledge
- Omnipresent in His location
- Omnipotent in His ability

This is our God! And His Son is the exact expression of His character and manifestation.

In His dealings with us, we learn from the scriptures that God is,

- Compassionate
- Gracious

- Righteous
- A sun and shield
- Impartial
- True
- Faithful

So to return to the question—*when should we stop believing God?*—the answer is that if we trust in who he *is,* we can never stop trusting Him. Not ever!

When the storm grows ever worse, we can and must still trust in the God that He says He is, even if His ways often baffle us entirely. He is the God in whom we can hope when all hope is gone. The one in whom faith is never misplaced. Our "God, that cannot lie" (Titus 1:2).

So, "Though he slay me, yet will I trust in him" (Job 13:15).

Have faith in God. (Mark 11:22)

49

HOW TO WITHSTAND IN THE EVIL DAY

Wherefore take unto you the whole armour of God, that ye may be able to withstand in the evil day, and having done all, to stand.
—Ephesians 6:13

Every believer is subject to regular spiritual bombardment, but from time to time, there comes a concentrated and vicious attack that seems to arrive out of nowhere. Both its suddenness and its ferocity are meant by the enemy to instill panic in the heart of the saint. This is what the scriptures refer to as "the evil day."

When Satan attacks through the world, it is always along the lines of 1 John 2:16:

The lust of the flesh, the lust of the eyes, and the pride of life. (See also Genesis 3:6.)

When the attack is a direct one, it seems random, but the aim is to overwhelm quickly and produce fear and a sense of being cutoff in the face of the assault. Job chapters 1 and 2 demonstrate this.

Understand that the enemy does not attack us in a disorganized or haphazard manner. The principalities, the powers, the rulers of the darkness of this age, the spiritual hosts of wickedness in the heavenly places (Ephesians 6:12) are motivated by an insatiable hatred of God and, by extension, us who are His. In this regard, the enemy is always seeking a season or opportunity (Luke 4:13) to launch the next, most effective attack.

We therefore need to put on "the whole armour of God" (Ephesians 6:10-18). This is one and the same as to "put . . . on the Lord Jesus Christ" (Romans 13:14). It is also identical to the admonition to "walk in the Spirit" (Galatians 5:16). If we abide in Christ (walking in the Spirit), we will have "put on the armour of light" (Romans 13:12) and be able to "withstand in the evil day, and having done all, to stand" (Ephesians 6:13).

Put simply, Satan's desire is to disrupt our walking in the Spirit so that we cannot live in the power of the Spirit. God's desire is that we may *stand*.

We need not fear the evil day, for our Good Shepherd has already gone before us and ordered our steps. He will prepare a table before us in the presence of our enemies, and our testimony will be,

When the wicked, even mine enemies and my foes, came upon me to eat up my flesh, they stumbled and fell. (Psalm 27:2)

David did not become brave, determined, and skilled on the day he met Goliath; he was already in possession of all these attributes. Hence, when that evil day came, he could step forth in the power of Yahweh and slay the enemy.

Similarly, we cannot wait until the giant is bearing down on us to suddenly become all that we should be. Now is the time to be prepared in the Spirit and stay prepared, for we know not when our evil day may come.

*Blessed be the L*ORD *my strength which teacheth my hands to war, and my fingers to fight. (Psalm 144:1)*

50

KEEP PRAYING

And he spake a parable unto them to this end, that men ought always to pray, and not to faint. —Luke 18:1

How quickly we faint when we do not quickly receive a response from the Lord.

We approach God as our Father in the name of His Son and make our petitions to Him, perhaps even adding, "according to your will," but in our minds, we have already formulated an idea of what we want from God and a time frame in which we want it. When that period of time expires and our urgent circumstance is now critical, but our prayers haven't been answered, what do we do then?

The options are two: *faint* (fall away in unbelief and panic) or *faith*. Note the words of the Master regarding faithful importunity:

Shall not God avenge his own elect, which cry day and night unto him, though he bear long with them? I tell you that he will avenge them speedily. (Luke 18:7-8)

We pray and pray and keep praying, then suddenly (speedily) God intervenes, and we stand in awe!

What was the reason for the delay? Only God knows the details in each circumstance, but one thing is sure: for the most part, the Lord was sanctifying and conforming the one who was waiting in prayer (1 Thessalonians 4:3).

Which matters more to us, the answer to our prayer (the transaction we seek) or the great, eternal work of sanctification (the transformation God seeks)? Once we have grasped the monumental truth that the Lord longs to fit us for the millennial reign, prayer takes on a different significance (Galatians 6:9). It genuinely becomes, "not my will, but thine, be done" (Luke 22:42). And what is His will? Our sanctification (plus, He promised to also supply all our needs).

For your heavenly Father knoweth that ye have need of all these things. But seek ye first the kingdom of God, and his righteousness; and all these things shall be added unto you. (Matthew 6:32-33)

51
TWELVE THINGS WE KNOW

*The secret things belong unto the L*ORD *our God: but those things which are revealed belong unto us and to our children forever, that we may do all the words of this law.* —**Deuteronomy 29:29**

There are many things that the Lord does not require us to know, but those things that we do need to know He has made abundantly clear. Here are twelve things we know about:

1. The work of Jesus.

   And we know *that the Son of God is come, and hath given us an understanding, that we may know him that is true, and we are in him that is true, even in his Son Jesus Christ. This is the true God, and eternal life. (1 John 5:20)*

2. Sin.

   We know *that whosoever is born of God sinneth not; but he that is begotten of God keepeth himself, and that wicked one toucheth him not. (1 John 5:18)*

3. Our spiritual standing.

   We know *that we have passed from death unto life, because we love the brethren. He that loveth not his brother abideth in death. (1 John 3:14)*

4. The truth.

   And hereby we know *that we are of the truth, and shall assure our hearts before him. (1 John 3:19)*

5. Having a loving heart.

   By this we know *that we love the children of God, when we love God, and keep his commandments. (1 John 5:2)*

6. The presence of God in us.

   And he that keepeth his commandments dwelleth in him, and he in him. And hereby we know *that he abideth in us, by the Spirit which he hath given us. (1 John 3:24)*

7. Our prayers.

   And if we know *that he hear us, whatsoever we ask, we know that we have the petitions that we desired of him. (1 John 5:15)*

8. The details of our lives.

    And we know *that all things work together for good to them that love God, to them who are the called according to his purpose.* (Romans 8:28)

9. The state of the elect and the world.

    And we know *that we are of God, and the whole world lieth in wickedness.* (1 John 5:19)

10. The unfolding environmental turmoil.

    For we know *that the whole creation groaneth and travaileth in pain together until now.* (Romans 8:22)

11. The last days.

    Little children, it is the last time: and as ye have heard that antichrist shall come, even now are there many antichrists; whereby we know *that it is the last time.* (1 John 2:18)

12. Our eternal future.

    For we know *that if our earthly house of this tabernacle were dissolved, we have a building of God, an house not made with hands, eternal in the heavens.* (2 Corinthians 5:1)

    Beloved, now are we the sons of God, and it doth not yet appear what we shall be: but we know *that, when he shall appear, we shall be like him; for we shall see him as he is.* (1 John 3:2)

There are a great many things that we do not know and, indeed, that we do not need to know, but let us hold fast to those things that have been revealed—things *we know.*

52

THE DANGER OF FALLING ASLEEP

And that, knowing the time, that now it is high time to awake out of sleep.
—Romans 13:11

We are at such risk of falling asleep spiritually that the Lord warns us repeatedly in scripture, leaving us in no doubt about our vulnerability.

In the Garden of Gethsemane, as our Lord returned from that agonizing time in prayer to the Father, we are told,

And he cometh unto the disciples, and findeth them asleep, and saith unto Peter, What, could ye not watch with me one hour? (Matthew 26:40)

The Lord's question to the disciples was not so much because they had fallen asleep physically but because they were in danger of falling asleep spiritually.

"Could ye not watch with me one hour?" That searching question is now directed as much to us as it was to Peter, James, and John on that momentous night. Those men (like so many of us) lacked the spiritual awareness to recognize what a critical hour they had slept through. How much have you and I missed because we could not watch with our Lord when it mattered most?

Watch and pray, that ye enter not into temptation. (Matthew 26:41a)

This was Jesus pleading with His disciples, knowing that His time with them was short, and desiring intensely that they understood that they must keep watching (being on the alert) and praying. Then, in just a few words, He explained to them the true nature of their battle:

The spirit indeed is willing, but the flesh is weak. (Matthew 26:41b)

And the flesh will always be weak, self-pampering, and independent of God. So what are we to do?

Therefore gird up the loins of your mind, be sober, and rest your hope fully upon the grace that is to be brought to you at the revelation of Jesus Christ. (1 Peter 1:13)

In other words, we have a choice as to whether or not we give way to the flesh:

Wherefore he saith, Awake thou that sleepest, and arise from the dead, and Christ shall give thee light. See then that ye walk circumspectly, not as fools, but as wise, redeeming the time, because the days are evil. Wherefore, be ye not unwise, but understanding what the will of the Lord is. (Ephesians 5:14-16)

We see then that the will of the Lord is that we wake up and stay awake!

But ye, brethren, are not in darkness, that that day should overtake you as a thief. Ye are all the children of light, and the children of the day: we are not of the night, nor of darkness. Therefore let us not sleep, as do others; but let us watch and be sober. For they that sleep sleep in the night; and they that be drunken are drunken in the night. But let us, who are of the day, be sober, putting on the breastplate of faith and love; and for an helmet, the hope of salvation. (1 Thessalonians 5:4-8)

We live in a day of such Laodicean self-satisfaction and ease—"I am rich, and increased with goods, and have need of nothing"—the ideal environment for a cozy, gratifying nap that extends into a slumber and eventually becomes a deep sleep (Revelation 3:17).

Can we not hear the warning of the scriptures?

How long wilt thou sleep, O sluggard? When wilt thou arise out of thy sleep? Yet a little sleep, a little slumber, a little folding of the hands to sleep. So shall thy poverty come as one that travelleth, and thy want as an armed man. (Proverbs 6:10-11)

What did the Lord say to the lukewarm, sleeping church of Laodicea?

[Thou] knowest not that thou art wretched, and miserable, and poor, and blind, and naked. (Revelation 3:17)

The thing about being lukewarm is that it is comfortable. Cold or hot environments tend to keep their occupants alert for survival's sake. But when our outlook and surroundings become lukewarm, sleep is almost inevitable.

Over and over again we are warned,

Do not love sleep, lest you become poor; open your eyes, and you will be satisfied with food. (Proverbs 20:13)

Oh, that we would open our eyes and be fed of the Lord with "the living bread which came down from heaven" (John 6:51)! But alas, so many of us are in the depths of such a profound sleep that we are in danger of becoming comatose.

Every time we fall asleep spiritually we miss something of tremendous importance, whether it is an opportunity to share in our Lord's suffering or, as in Luke 9:28–32, to behold His glory. We lose moments and opportunities that will never come again in this life.

May the "wise virgins" shake themselves awake from their slumber and trim their lamps, for the Bridegroom cometh (Matthew 25)!

MORE FROM
INNOVO PUBLISHING

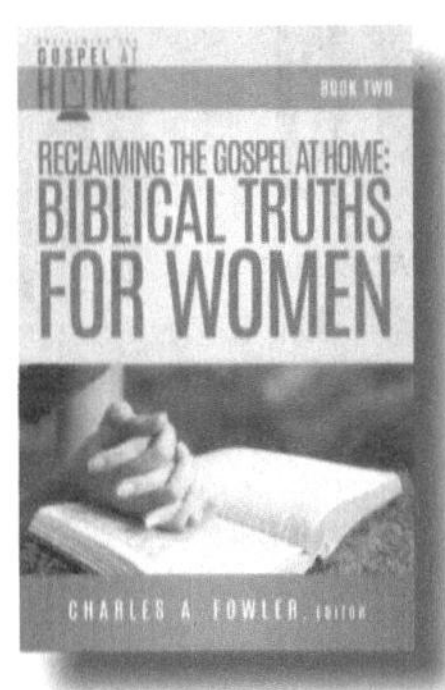